English In motion

3 Workbook

Gill Holley
Rob Metcalf

Richmond PUBLISHING

Contents

WELCOME Reference

GRAMMAR

Present simple

Affirmative
I sing. You sing. He sings. She sings. It sings.
We sing. You sing. They sing.

Negative	
Full form	Contracted form
I do not sing. You do not sing. He does not sing. She does not sing. It does not sing.	I don't sing. You don't sing. He doesn't sing. She doesn't sing. It doesn't sing.
We do not sing. You do not sing. They do not sing.	We don't sing. You don't sing. They don't sing.

Questions
Do I sing? Do you sing? Does he sing? Does she sing? Does it sing?
Do we sing? Do you sing? Do they sing?

Short answers	
Affirmative	Negative
Yes, I do. Yes, you do. Yes, he does. Yes, she does. Yes, it does.	No, I don't. No, you don't. No, he doesn't. No, she doesn't. No, it doesn't.
Yes, we do. Yes, you do. Yes, they do.	No, we don't. No, you don't. No, they don't.

- See present simple use on page 9.

1 Three of the questions are wrong. Correct them.

1. What club do he goes to?
   What club does he go to?
2. What music do you like?
   ______
3. Which do your favourite film be?
   ______
4. Which badges do you collect?
   ______
5. What's your sister's name?
   ______
6. How often does your aunt visits?
   ______

→ **Answers** page 116

like/not like + *-ing* form

- We can use this structure to talk about likes and dislikes.
  I **like reading**.
  Simon **doesn't like playing** football.
- See *-ing* spelling rules on page 8.

2 Complete the sentences about Laura's and Steve's likes and dislikes.

	play the guitar	travel to other countries	go to the cinema	ride a bike
Laura	✗	✓	✓	✗
Steve	✗	✓	✗	✓

1 Laura and Steve *don't like playing* the guitar.
2 Laura ______________ a bike.
3 Steve and Laura ______________ to other countries.
4 Steve ______________ to the cinema.
5 Steve ______________ a bike.
6 Laura ______________ the guitar.

➟ **Answers** page 116

Past simple

Affirmative
I talked.
You talked.
He talked.
She talked.
It talked.
We talked.
You talked.
They talked.

Negative	
Full form	Contracted form
I did not talk.	I didn't talk.
You did not talk.	You didn't talk.
He did not talk.	He didn't talk.
She did not talk.	She didn't talk.
It did not talk.	It didn't talk.
We did not talk.	We didn't talk.
You did not talk.	You didn't talk.
They did not talk.	They didn't talk.

Questions
Did I talk?
Did you talk?
Did he talk?
Did she talk?
Did it talk?
Did we talk?
Did you talk?
Did they talk?

Short answers	
Affirmative	Negative
Yes, I did.	No, I didn't.
Yes, you did.	No, you didn't.
Yes, he did.	No, he didn't.
Yes, she did.	No, she didn't.
Yes, it did.	No, it didn't.
Yes, we did.	No, we didn't.
Yes, you did.	No, you didn't.
Yes, they did.	No, they didn't.

- See past simple use on page 32.

3 Write the past simple questions and answers.

1 **A** Where / you / go on holiday?
Where did you go on holiday?

2 **B** I / go / to Disneyland
____

3 **A** Who / be / with you?
____

4 **B** My parents / be / there
____

5 **A** What / they / think of Disneyland?
____

6 **B** They / not like / it
____

➟ **Answers** page 116

WELCOME

VOCABULARY – Personal things

1 Write the names of Lauren's personal things.

1	l*ist*	**5**	l_ _ _ _ _ _
2	t_ _ _ _ _ c_ _ _	**6**	c_ _ _ _ _ t_ _ _ _ _
3	C_	**7**	i_ _ _ _ _ _ _ _ _ _
4	s_ _ _ _ _	**8**	p_ _ _ _ _ _ _

GRAMMAR

Present simple

2 Correct the information about Lauren.

Lauren's 15 years old and she lives in London, England. She loves animals and she's got two pets, a cat and a dog. She's interested in the theatre. She likes music too and she plays the guitar. On Saturday she's going to Zach's birthday party.

1 *She doesn't live in London. She lives in Birmingham.*

2 ______________________

3 ______________________

4 ______________________

5 ______________________

3 Write questions for the answers.

1 What *does she collect* ?

She collects stamps.

2 How many ______________________________ ?

She's got two pets.

3 How ______________________________ ?

She goes to school by bus.

4 What ______________________________ ?

She likes science fiction films.

5 Where ______________________________ ?

She's going shopping.

Past simple

4 Complete with past simple of the verbs.

not be buy sunbathe not buy
see ~~spend~~ take put

I (1) *spent* my summer holiday at Caernarfon in North Wales with my parents and my sister, Jane. We (2) ______ the castle and (3) ______ a lot of photos. The weather (4) ______ very good but one day we (5) ______ on the beach. I (6) ______ any souvenirs, but I (7) ______ this postcard and (8) ______ it on my corkboard.

5 Write questions in the past simple. Then answer them.

1 Where / go / in the summer ?
Where did you go in the summer?

2 How long / stay ?

____

____

3 What / do ?

____

____

4 be / the weather / good ?

____

____

5 buy / any souvenirs ?

____

____

ENGLISH YOU NEED

6 Complete the sentences.

1 You can learn a lot of English from *song lyrics.*

2 If you read in English, it ______________________________

3 You can practise your English with ______________________________

4 You can read English words every day on ______________________________

5 A fun way to learn new words is to ______________________________

FIRST IMPRESSIONS

GRAMMAR

like + *-ing* form

- We use *like* and other verbs, such as *love*, *hate*, *not mind* and *can't stand* + *-ing* form to talk about preferences.

✗✗✗	✗✗	✗
can't stand	hate	not like
✓	✓✓	✓✓✓
not mind	like	love

Spelling rules: *-ing* form

Most verbs	talk try	+ *-ing*	talking trying
Verbs ending *-e*	use take	change *-e* to *-ing*	using taking
Verbs ending *-ie*	die tie	change *-ie* to *-y* + *-ing*	dying tying
Verbs ending consonant + vowel + consonant	forget swim	double consonant + *-ing*	forgetting swimming

1 Look at the table and complete the sentences. Use *love*, *like*, *don't mind*, *don't like*, *hate* and *can't stand* + *-ing* form.

1 Dawn *loves following* (follow) fashion. ✓✓✓
2 Anya __________ (follow) fashion. ✗✗✗
3 Dawn __________ (create) her own style. ✓
4 Anya __________ (create) her own style. ✗
5 Dawn and Anya __________ (wear) jewellery. ✓✓
6 Dawn __________ (shop) in small shops. ✗✗

➡ **Answers** page 116

Present simple v. present continuous

Present simple

- See present simple forms on page 4.
- We add *-s* to the third person singular form.

Edward **wears** glasses.

Spelling rules: third person singular

Most verbs	run eat	+ *-s*	runs eats
Verbs ending *-s*, *-x*, *-ch*, *-o*	watch go	+ *-es*	watches goes
Verbs ending consonant + *-y*	fly try	change *-y* to *-ies*	flies tries
Irregular verbs	be have	irregular	is has

Present continuous

Affirmative	
Full form	**Contracted form**
I am looking. You are looking. He is looking. She is looking. It is looking.	I'm looking. You're looking. He's looking. She's looking. It's looking.
We are looking. You are looking. They are looking.	We're looking. You're looking. They're looking.

Negative	
Full form	**Contracted form**
I am not looking. You are not looking. He is not looking. She is not looking. It is not looking.	I'm not looking. You aren't looking. He isn't looking. She isn't looking. It isn't looking.
We are not looking. You are not looking. They are not looking.	We aren't looking. You aren't looking. They aren't looking.

Questions
Am I looking? Are you looking? Is he looking? Is she looking? Is it looking?
Are we looking? Are you looking? Are they looking?

Short answers	
Affirmative	**Negative**
Yes, I am. Yes, you are. Yes, he is. Yes, she is. Yes, it is.	No, I'm not. No, you aren't. No, he isn't. No, she isn't. No, it isn't.
Yes, we are. Yes, you are. Yes, they are.	No, we aren't. No, you aren't. No, they aren't.

- We form the present continuous with the verb *be* and the *-ing* form of the main verb.
  Paula **is talking** on the phone.

- We use the present continuous and present simple for different situations.

Present simple
For routines and habits. Samantha **washes** her hair daily.
For facts and things that are always true. December **isn't** a warm month in Europe.
With adverbs of frequency and other frequency expressions. I **go** to the park **every day**.
With state and sense verbs, e.g. *like*, *love*, *hate*, *want*, *know*, etc. We **like** tea. NOT We ~~are liking~~ tea.

Present continuous
For things that are happening now. **I'm talking** to John now.
With time expressions like *now*, *at the moment*. She**'s listening** to music **at the moment**.

Present continuous for future plans

- We can also use the present continuous for planned future arrangements, usually with a future time expression.
  Paul**'s coming** for dinner **tomorrow**.

2 Circle the correct option.

1 My brother *works* / *is working* in New York next week.
2 *Are you going* / *Do you go* shopping very often?
3 *I go* / *'m going* to Brazil next year.
4 Mark *drives* / *is driving* to work everyday.
5 Paul *isn't liking* / *doesn't like* sport very much.
6 Margaret, you can switch off the TV. *I'm not watching* / *don't watch* it.

→ **Answers** page 116

Comparatives and superlatives

Spelling rules

		Comparative	Superlative
Short adjective small	+ *-er/-est*	smaller	the smallest
Adjective ending in *-e* large	+ *-r/-st*	larger	the largest
Short adjective ending in vowel + consonant, except *-w* big	double the consonant + *-er/-est*	bigger	the biggest
Adjective of two or more syllables modern	*more/most* + adjective	more modern	the most modern
Adjective ending in consonant + *-y* early	change *-y* to *-i* + *-er/-est*	earlier	the earliest
Irregular adjective good bad	Irregular	better worse	the best the worst

Comparatives

- We use comparative adjectives to compare two people, animals or things.
  Anna is **taller** than Tina.
- We follow the comparative adjective with *than*, not *that*.
  Anna is taller **than** Tina.
  NOT Anna is taller ~~that~~ Tina.

Superlatives

- We use superlative adjectives to compare three or more people, animals or things.
  Anna is **the tallest** in her class.
- When we use superlatives, we can say *in the world* or *in the class*. We don't say *of the world*, etc.
  Who is the richest person **in** the world?
  NOT Who is the richest person ~~of~~ the world?

3 Complete the table.

Adjective	Comparative	Superlative
(1) *tall*	taller	the tallest
late	(2) ______	(3) ______
hot	(4) ______	the hottest
hungry	hungrier	(5) ______
beautiful	(6) ______ ______	the most beautiful

➟ **Answers** page 116

What ... like?

- When we want to ask someone to describe a person, thing or place, we use *What ... like?*
  What are the shops **like**?
- We generally use *How is/How are* to ask about someone's health.
  How is Jane these days?
- We don't use the contracted form *'re* after *What*.
  NOT ~~What're~~ the shops like?
- Don't confuse *What's* + subject + *like?* with *What does* + subject + *like?*
  What's Kate **like**? She's very pretty.
  What does Kate **like**? She likes coffee.

4 Four of the questions are wrong. Correct them.

1 What~~'re~~ those cakes like?
What are those cakes like?

2 How is Paul? He's got dark hair.
______

3 What's the food like in London?

____

4 What does the weather like in Paris now?

____

5 What are the Johnson family like?

____

6 What's the new baby likes?

____

➞ **Answers** page 116

VOCABULARY

Student's Multi-ROM Speaking dictionary

Fashion

belt	/belt/	______
boots	/buːts/	______
earrings	/ˈɪərɪŋz/	______
headband	/ˈhedbænd/	______
hoodie	/ˈhʊdi/	______
leggings	/ˈlegɪŋz/	______
necklace	/ˈnekləs/	______
ring	/rɪŋ/	______
shirt	/ʃɜːt/	______
sweatshirt	/ˈswetʃɜːt/	______
tie	/taɪ/	______
trousers	/ˈtraʊzəz/	______

Cities: adjectives

crowded	/ˈkraʊdɪd/	______
empty	/ˈempti/	______
industrial	/ɪnˈdʌstriəl/	______
lively	/ˈlaɪvli/	______
peaceful	/ˈpiːsfl/	______
polluted	/pəˈluːtɪd/	______
touristy	/ˈtʊərɪsti/	______
ugly	/ˈʌgli/	______

English you need

- Start a conversation

Hi. What's your name?

____

Is this your first trip to England?

____

What do you think of Manchester?

____

What's the weather like in Seville?

____

And what's Seville like?

____

What subjects do you like studying?

____

Do you like learning English?

____

Learning tip

- When you learn new adjectives, notice the different suffixes.

1 Write the adjective suffixes. Then find more adjectives with these suffixes.

-ive -ful -ic -y -ed -ous

1 touristy	4 danger_
2 pollut_	5 authent_
3 expens_	6 peace_

____

____

➞ **Answers** page 116

1 FIRST IMPRESSIONS

VOCABULARY – Fashion

1 Find clothes in the puzzle. Then look at the pictures and write them in the table.

brtnagaposheadbandos
ihoodiednecklacet(shirt)y
notrousersirtieareboots t
shorleggingstrobeltroup
ipearringsrsweatshirthip

A	1 shirt	5 ________	9 ________
B	2 ________	11 ________	
C	3 ________	4 ________	10 ________
D	6 ________	7 ________	
E	8 ________		

2 Find categories A–E in the box.

bottoms short-sleeved ~~tops~~ jewellery short accessories tight footwear baggy

A tops **B** ________ **C** ________ **D** ________ **E** ________

3 Complete the descriptions with the other words in exercise 2.

Jack's going to wear a (1) ________ - ________ shirt.

Ana's going to wear (2) ________ trousers.

Andrea's going to wear a (3) ________ T-shirt.

GRAMMAR

like + *-ing* form

1 Complete with a verb from each box.

not mind ~~like~~	listen be
hate can't stand	buy ~~dress~~
not like love	wear go

Jack (1) *likes dressing* smartly, and he (2) ________ ties for his collection. He's got thirty! But he (3) ________ jeans. He hasn't got any. He (4) ________ shopping on Saturdays, but he prefers weekdays because they're quieter and he (5) ________ in places with a lot of people. He's into jazz music, and he (6) ________ to pop.

Present simple v. present continuous

2 Write the present simple or present continuous of the verbs in the article.

buy prepare not wear ~~talk~~ not follow work

The fashion column

It's Saturday lunchtime, and I (**1**) *'m talking* to Tina Wayfield. Tina (**2**) ________ for a teen magazine, and she (**3**) ________ an article about fashion trends this winter.

When I see Tina, I get a surprise. She (**4**) ________ any trendy clothes. 'I (**5**) ________ fashion,' she says. 'I love looking around shops, but I always (**6**) ________ similar clothes. I feel most comfortable in jeans and a top.' Apparently, most designers like simple clothes.

3 Write questions. Use the present simple or present continuous.

1 **A** *Are you watching* (watch) the match?
B Yes. The score's 1–0 at the moment.

2 **A** What ________ (do)?
B I'm a student.

3 **A** Why ________ (look) in my bag?
B Sorry! I thought it was my bag.

4 **A** Where ________ (live)?
B My penfriend? In Vienna, in Austria.

5 **A** ________ (rain)?
B No, it's sunny.

6 **A** ________ (like) tattoos?
B No. I think they're horrible!

Present continuous for future plans

4 Write about your future plans.

1 *I'm visiting my grandparents on Sunday afternoon.*

2 ________

3 ________

4 ________

5 ________

6 ________

VOCABULARY Cities: adjectives

1 Write three adjectives to describe each of the places.

This place was (1) b*eautiful*______! The beach was (2) e__________, and it was really (3) p__________

This place was quite (7) u__________. It was (8) m__________ and (9) t__________. We didn't like it much.

What a shock! The city was very (4) i__________. It was also (5) c__________ and (6) p__________

This was our favourite place. It was so (10) e__________! With people from all over the world, it was (11) c______________ and really (12) l__________

2 Complete the description of your city, town or village.

I live in ____________________ in ____________________. I think it's ____________________ and ____________________ here. My favourite place is ____________________ because it's ____________________ and ____________________. But I don't like ____________________ because it's ____________________ and ____________________

1

GRAMMAR

Comparatives and superlatives

1 Write comparatives and *than* if necessary.

big good crowded expensive ~~safe~~

1. A village is *safer than* a city because there's less crime.
2. The shops in a city are ______ in a village, so you can find everything you need there.
3. But prices are generally higher, so a city is ______ a village.
4. Public transport in a city is ______ in a village, especially in the rush hour.
5. On balance, I think that village life is ______ life in a city.

2 Write the superlative adjective in the correct place in the advert.

cheap fine famous cosmopolitan ~~big~~

Harrods, London

With its 18,000 m² of shopping space and 330 departments, Harrods is the (1) *biggest* department store in the world. The workers come from fifty different countries, so it's one of the (2) ______ stores in the world, too. This exclusive store sells clothes, furniture, food – everything of the (3) ______ quality. And some of the (4) ______ people in the country are customers, including the British Royal Family. Harrods isn't the (5) ______ store though; it costs ten euros just to park your car!

3 Compare the cities. Use comparative and superlative adjectives.

	London	New York	Sao Paulo
large	✓	✓✓	✓✓✓
hot	✓	✓✓	✓✓✓
dry	✓✓✓	✓✓	✓
expensive	✓✓✓	✓✓	✓

1. *New York is larger than London, but Sao Paulo is the largest.*
2. ______
3. ______
4. ______

What ... like?

4 Complete the conversation.

A If you go to Morocco, you really must visit Marrakech.
B Really? Why? What (1) *'s Marrakech like*?
A It's great. There are a lot of markets.
B What (2) ______?
A They're very lively. And there's a big square in the centre.
B What (3) ______?
A It's always busy. People go there to eat the local food.
B What (4) ______?
A It's delicious. You should also try the tea.
B Why? What (5) ______?
A It's mint tea, with a lot of sugar. And you'll meet lots of people.
B What (6) ______?
A They're very friendly, very hospitable.

READING

1 What do people buy in markets where you live? Tick (✓) the things.

clothes ___ food ___ jewellery ___ books ___ souvenirs ___

2 Read about London markets. Which thing in exercise 1 isn't in the descriptions?

Answer: ______________

London markets

London's full of exciting things to do, but if you want to get an impression of how Londoners live, visit one of its markets. Here's a small selection.

Portobello Road

This famous market was the location for the popular film *Notting Hill*. On Saturdays, the market sells antiques, jewellery, clothes and souvenirs. A section in the middle sells fruit and vegetables every day of the week. It's quite touristy and can get crowded, but it's always lively.

Covent Garden

The name Covent Garden comes from the Middle Ages, when the Convent of St. Peter maintained a large vegetable garden. The original market sold fruit and vegetables, but today it only sells crafts, jewellery and clothes six days a week, and antiques on Mondays. A lot of people come for its atmosphere, with cafés, restaurants and performances by buskers and other street artists.

Borough Market

Although it's less famous than Portobello Road and Covent Garden, it has the longest history, and is one of the country's largest food markets. Open on Friday and Saturday, you can buy food from around the world. It's also famous for its beautiful Victorian architecture, and was a location for the third Harry Potter film.

3 Write the name of the market – PB (Portobello Road), CG (Covent Garden) or BM (Borough Market).

1 It isn't open every day. BM
2 It sells the largest variety of things. ____
3 It doesn't appear in a popular film. ____
4 It's the oldest. ____
5 It sells food and clothes. ____
6 It sold different things in the past. ____

4 Match the words and expressions with the definitions.

1 antiques		**a** used, not new
2 second-hand		**b** street musicians
3 the Middle Ages		**c** old objects
4 crafts		**d** hand-made objects
5 buskers		**e** 400 to 1500 AD

1

ENGLISH YOU NEED

1 Complete the dialogue with words in the box. You can use the words more than once.

like languages think trip is do what study what's

A Hi, I'm Petra.
B I'm Jean. I'm Peter's cousin from Paris.
A Right! (1) ___Is___ this your first ___trip___ to England?
B No, it isn't. I came two years ago.
A (2) ________ ________ you ________ of London?
B I love it. There's a lot to see here.
A (3) ________ Paris ________?
B It's big, and very beautiful.
A And (4) ________ the weather ________ there?
B It's cold and wet right now.
A Your English is very good.
B Thanks. I have a good teacher. (5) ________ ________ ________ you ________ at school?
A I study German.
B I study German too!
A We should practise together. (6) ________ you ________ shopping?
B I don't mind it. Why?
A We're going to Portobello Market tomorrow morning. Do you want to come?
B OK.

LISTENING

2 1 Listen to Petra and Jean. What are they comparing?

1 Expressions in English and French
2 Paris and London
3 Two markets

Answer: _____

3 1 Listen again. Circle the correct option.

1 Jean's opinion of Portobello Road is *positive* / *positive and negative*.
2 To buy the best things, you need to arrive *early* / *late* in the morning.
3 The world's biggest antiques market's in *London* / *Paris*.
4 The expression 'flea market' *exists* / *doesn't exist* in French.
5 The market in Paris is more *serious* / *touristy*.
6 *Portobello Road* / *The Paris market* sells everything.

DICTATION

4 2 Listen. Write six sentences about Petra.

1 She ________________
2 ________________
3 ________________
4 ________________
5 ________________
6 ________________

WRITING – My views on fashion

1 Write the words in **bold** in the correct place.

1. I love my leggings **new**.
   I love my new leggings.
2. **Sporty clothes** I prefer.
   ____
3. Everyone's **these days** wearing dark colours.
   ____
4. I wear **usually** leggings.
   ____
5. I wear **to school** leggings and a sweatshirt.
   ____
6. I'm wearing my headband **orange**.
   ____

Word order

2 Read the letter. Check your answers

Dear Auntie May,
This letter is to say thank you for my birthday present.

I love my new leggings and headband. As you know, I prefer sporty clothes, and these are perfect for me. I like the colours too. Everyone's wearing dark colours these days, but I think they're boring. Personally, I like red and orange.

We haven't got a school uniform so I usually wear leggings and a sweatshirt to school. At the moment, I'm wearing my new red leggings, a baggy sweatshirt, and my orange headband. I took a photo so you can see. They look great! Thanks again,
Karen

3 Write a letter to a relative. Say thank you for a present of clothes.

Dear ____________,
This letter is ______________________
____
I love my new ______________________
As you know, I prefer ______________________
____
Everyone's wearing ______________________
but I think ______________________
Personally, I like ______________________
I usually wear ______________________
____
At the moment, I'm wearing ______________________
____
Thanks again,
____

CORRECTION

4 Correct the sentences.

1. I can't stand wear jewellery. ✗
   I can't stand wearing jewellery.
2. I'm not usually following fashion. ✗
   ____
3. I'm wearing some jeans baggy now. ✗
   ____
4. Clothes in small shops are more cheap. ✗
   ____
5. What do the shops like where you live? ✗
   ____
6. The most busy time is on Saturday. ✗
   ____

SELF CHECK

1

Clothes

1 Complete the words. _ / 5

1 Paul usually wears a shirt, tie and t _ _ _ _ _ _ _
2 I often wear a l _ _ _ - s _ _ _ _ _ _ T-shirt.
3 My sister loves collecting jewellery, especially e _ _ _ _ _ _ _
4 Is it 'in' to wear jeans with a b _ _ _?
5 My favourite tops are hoodies or s _ _ _ _ _ _ _ _ _ _

Usually and now

2 Write the verbs in the present simple or present continuous. _ / 5

play come study not have give

Hi! How are things? We started school again three weeks ago. I'm in my third year now, so I (1) ______________ a lot at the moment. Our English teacher (2) ______________ us homework every evening! I (3) ______________ time to go out during the week but I always (4) ______________ volleyball on Saturdays.
Next Sunday's my birthday and some friends (5) ______________ to my place for a barbecue. Can you come too?

Describe a place

3 Write the comparative or superlative form of the adjectives. _ / 5

cosmopolitan clean lively peaceful wet

I live in Liverpool but this summer we stayed at a village in Ireland. The countryside was green because it rains a lot, in fact it's the (1) ______________ place in the country. It was very quiet there, (2) ______________ than Liverpool. And the air was (3) ______________. But there are more things to do in Liverpool and it's (4) ______________. People from all over the world live here too. It's one of the (5) ______________ cities in England.

Start a conversation

4 Circle the correct option. _ / 5

A This your first visit to England, Kostas. What do you think (1) *in / of* our school?
B It's different from my school in Athens.
A What (2) *'s / does* your school like?
B Well, we don't wear a uniform. But I'm improving my English here.
A (3) *Are / Do* you like learning English?
B Yes, I do. And it's necessary. A lot of tourists visit Greece in summer.
A (4) *Are / Do* people like the tourists?
B Yes, I think so. Tourism is important for our economy.
A What (5) *are / do* people like in Greece?
B They're very friendly and hospitable.

Clothes and fashion

5 Complete the words. _ / 5

I love clothes but I don't really (1) f______________ fashion. I like creating my own style. I usually wear a long skirt and a top. I don't (2) m______________ jeans, but everybody wears them and I prefer to look different. I love (3) w______________ jewellery so I've got a lot of necklaces and rings. I like (4) s______________ for clothes in markets because you can find more original things there. And I can't (5) s______________ going to big shops, because they're crowded.

➞ **Answers** page 118

2 Reference

TEAM WORK

GRAMMAR

have to/not have to

Affirmative
I have to You have to He has to She has to It has to
We have to You have to They have to

Negative	
Full form	Contracted form
I do not have to You do not have to He does not have to She does not have to It does not have to	I don't have to You don't have to He doesn't have to She doesn't have to It doesn't have to
We do not have to You do not have to They do not have to	We don't have to You don't have to They don't have to go

- We use *have to* to express an obligation. *Have to* is not as strong as *must*. We often use *have to* for actions that are necessary because of circumstances, not because of a rule or an order.
  I **have to take** two buses to school.
  I **must go** home now – it's getting late.
- We use *not have to* to express an absence of obligation, not a prohibition.
  We **don't have to go** to school tomorrow.
  We **mustn't play** near the railway line.

1 Write the sentences. Use *have to, has to, don't have to* or *doesn't have to*.

1 I / not go to bed early / at the weekend
I don't have to go to bed early at the weekend.

2 My dad / drive over 200 kilometres / every day
______

3 Students at my school / learn German and French
______

4 People / not wear a uniform / in many jobs
______

5 A film star / not wait / at the bus stop
______

6 Most people / work hard all their lives
______

➟ **Answers** page 116

have to: questions

Questions
Do I have to go?
Do you have to go?
Does he have to go?
Does she have to go?
Does it have to go?
Do we have to go?
Do you have to go?
Do they have to go?

Short answers	
Affirmative	Negative
Yes, I do.	No, I don't.
Yes, you do.	No, you don't.
Yes, he does.	No, he doesn't.
Yes, she does.	No, she doesn't.
Yes, it does.	No, it doesn't.
Yes, we do.	No, we don't.
Yes, you do.	No, you don't.
Yes, they do.	No, they don't.

- In questions, *have to* expresses obligation due to circumstances.
  Does Sean **have to** repair the computer now?
- We use question words to make *wh*-questions.
  What time **do** you **have to go** to bed during the week?
- In short answers, we repeat the auxiliary *do*/*does*.
  Do you **have to share** your bedroom?
  Yes, I **do**.
  NOT Yes, I ~~have (to).~~

2 Match the questions with the correct answers.

1 Do women have to wear hats in church? — b
2 Does your passport have to include your photo?
3 What do motorcyclists have to wear on their heads?
4 Does a digital camera have to use film?
5 Do you have to have a licence to drive a bicycle in the UK?
6 What do you have to do for homework?

a Crash helmets.
b No, they don't.
c Read a book.
d No, you don't.
e Yes, it does.
f No, it doesn't.

➡ **Answers** page 116

can, can't/mustn't, not have to

- We often use *can*/*can't* + infinitive to talk about ability.
  I **can swim** very well.
- However, we can also use *can* to ask for and to give permission.
  Can I **borrow** your newspaper?
- We can use *can't* to refuse permission or to express prohibition.
  You **can't play** football here. Look at the sign.
- We also use *mustn't* to express prohibition.
  You **mustn't swim** in the canal. It's dangerous.
- We use *not have to* to express an absence of obligation.
  You **don't have to come** with us if you don't want to.

3 Read the leaflet. Then complete the sentences with *can*, *can't*, *mustn't* and *not have to*.

> # Join our activity week in the Yorkshire Dales for children aged 11-16
>
> Activities include caving, trekking, rafting and mountain biking, but we won't force you to do anything you don't want! If you are taller than 1.65m, try rafting.
> The price includes everything, but lunch is an optional extra.
> We prohibit video games on the camp grounds.
> Parents: don't worry about your children's safety! All our monitors are fully trained.

1 Children *can* try a range of exciting activities.
2 Children ____________ do all the activities.
3 Children under 1.65m ____________ go rafting.
4 Children ____________ have lunch.
5 Children ____________ bring their video games.
6 Parents ____________ worry about their children's safety.

➟ **Answers** page 116

VOCABULARY

Student's Multi-ROM Speaking dictionary

Helping at home

mop the floor	/mɒp ðə flɔː/	____________
clear the table	/klɪə ðə 'teɪbl/	____________
do the ironing	/duː ðə 'aɪənɪŋ/	____________
do the washing	/duː ðə 'wɒʃɪŋ/	____________
do the washing-up	/duː ðə wɒʃɪŋ'ʌp/	____________
hang out the washing	/hæŋ aʊt ðə 'wɒʃɪŋ/	____________
lay the table	/leɪ ðə 'teɪbl/	____________
make your bed	/meɪk jə bed/	____________
take out the rubbish	/teɪk aʊt ðə 'rʌbɪʃ/	____________
tidy your room	/'taɪdi jə ruːm/	____________

Adventure activities

canoeing	/kə'nuːɪŋ/	____________
caving	/'keɪvɪŋ/	____________
horse riding	/hɔːs 'raɪdɪŋ/	____________
mountain biking	/'maʊntən 'baɪkɪŋ/	____________
rafting	/'rɑːftɪŋ/	____________
rock climbing	/rɒk 'klaɪmɪŋ/	____________
snowboarding	/'snəʊbɔːdɪŋ/	____________
trekking	/'trekɪŋ/	____________

English you need

- Use teen talk

How's it going?

____

What are you up to?

____

Hang on.

____

Do you fancy going to the cinema?

____

Sure! Why not?

____

No way!

____

There are loads of interesting films.

____

Learning tip

- Choosing the best and worst things in a category can help you remember new words.

1 Rank these activities, from the best (1) to the worst (10).

_ tidy your room
_ make your bed
_ lay the table
_ mop the floor
_ do the washing
_ horse riding
_ rafting
_ canoeing
_ caving
_ trekking

2 Make a list of the two best and the two worst things in these categories.

Types of TV programmes

The best:

____

The worst:

____

Music genres

The best:

____

The worst:

____

Forms of transport

The best:

____

The worst:

____

→ **Answers** page 116

2 TEAM WORK

VOCABULARY – Helping at home

1 What housework do Tom and Tina have to do? Write instructions.

~~do~~ tidy clear do
mop take out do lay
hang out make

your bed ~~the ironing~~ the washing the floor
your room the washing the rubbish the table
the washing-up the table

1

2

3

4

5

6

7

8

9

10

1 *Do the ironing.*
2 __________
3 __________
4 __________
5 __________
6 __________
7 __________
8 __________
9 __________
10 __________

2 Write about the housework you do. Use frequency words and expressions.

never hardly ever sometimes often every day
once / twice a week three times a month

I often take out the rubbish.

GRAMMAR

have to/not have to

1 Look at the school information. Then match the parts of the sentences.

Midfield school

Clothes	no uniform, but no trainers
Lunch	in the school canteen or at home
Sports	every Wednesday (football or hockey)
Times	9.00am – 4.10pm

1 You have to wear *d*
2 You don't have to wear _
3 You have to play _
4 You don't have to play _
5 You have to be _
6 You don't have to stay _

a a uniform.
b at school for lunch.
c in school at 9 o'clock.
d shoes, not trainers.
e football.
f a sport.

2 Look at the information. Write true sentences about England and France.

	England	France
have an identity card	✗	✓
buy a TV licence	✓	✗
be 16 to ride a moped (=very small motorbike)	✓	✗

An English person …

1 *doesn't have to have an identity card.*
2 ____________________
3 ____________________

A French person …

4 ____________________
5 ____________________
6 ____________________

have to: questions

3 Write questions with *have to*. Then answer the questions.

1 astronauts / wear / a uniform ?
Do astronauts have to wear a uniform?
No, they don't, but they wear a special suit.

2 how many years / pupils / go / Primary school ?
____

3 teachers / be / an expert in their subject ?
____

4 what / a receptionist / do ?
____

5 you / sing / well / to be a pop star ?
____

6 how often / footballers / train ?
____

VOCABULARY Adventure activities

1 Write the names of the activities.

1 t r e k k i n g

2 c _ v _ n _

3 m _ u _ t _ i _ - b _ k _ n _

4 r _ f _ i _ g

5 h _ r _ e - r _ d _ n _

6 s _ o _ b _ a _ d _ n _

7 r _ c _ c _ i _ b _ n _

8 c _ n _ e _ n _

2 Complete the sentences for you.

1. In my opinion, the most exciting activity is ____________________
2. I think ____________________ is very dangerous.
3. I'd like to try ____________________
4. But I never want to go ____________________
5. I think ____________________ is a popular activity in my country.
6. But not many people go ____________________

GRAMMAR

can, can't/mustn't, not have to

3 Choose a sentence with a similar meaning.

1. We have permission to sleep outside.
   - a We don't have to sleep outside.
   - b We can't sleep outside.
   - c We can sleep outside. ✓
2. It's forbidden to leave the camp.
   - a You can leave the camp.
   - b You mustn't leave the camp.
   - c You don't have to leave the camp.
3. It isn't necessary to do all the activities.
   - a You can do all the activities.
   - b You mustn't do all the activities.
   - c You don't have to do all the activities.
4. It isn't permitted to swim here.
   - a You can swim here.
   - b You can't swim here.
   - c You don't have to swim here.

4 Write *can* or *mustn't* in the sentences about snowboarding.

1. You __can__ go snowboarding in most ski areas.
2. You ________ do it without special equipment.
3. You ________ use the ski lift, but be careful when you get off.
4. You ________ go snowboarding 'off piste' – it's very dangerous.
5. You ________ stop and rest in the middle of the 'piste'.
6. You ________ practise your jumps in special areas.

5 Circle the correct option.

Rochbach Riding Camp

We offer riding classes every morning. In the afternoon, beginners (1) (can) / *can't* practise in the school. More advanced riders (2) *mustn't* / *can* go on treks.

Important:
Students (3) *mustn't* / *can* bring mobile phones – they are forbidden at the camp. In the case of emergencies, parents (4) *can* / *mustn't* phone the school director but they (5) *can* / *can't* visit more than once a week. We have a canteen for meals but you (6) *can* / *mustn't* take food to the cabins.

6 Write sentences with *mustn't* or *don't have to* and a verb.

drive drink make wear ~~pay~~ have

1. You __don't have to pay__ to go in.
2. You ________________ fast.
3. You ________________ a noise.
4. You ________________ experience.
5. You ________________ the water.
6. You ________________ formal clothes.

7 Write sentences with *can*, *can't/mustn't* or *don't have to* about your country.

use a mobile   have a TV licence
start work   pay for secondary education
ride a motorbike   ~~drink and drive~~

1. *You mustn't drink and drive.*
2. ________________
3. ________________
4. ________________
5. ________________
6. ________________

READING

1 Which areas do you and your parent(s) disagree about the most? Write 1 (the most) to 5 (the least).

_ housework _ bad language
_ your clothes _ going out
_ homework

2 Read the article. Write the best heading above each section.

No exceptions! Put it on paper
~~A new solution~~ Let's talk about it
What happens if ...?

Family contracts

A *A new solution*

Relationships between parents and teenagers can sometimes be difficult. Communication is often a problem as well as differences of opinion about rules and rights.
Some families, especially in the USA, are using family contracts to try to solve these differences. How do they work?

B ____________

The first step is for the family to talk about rules together. These can cover areas like behaviour, doing housework, homework, clothes and appearance. A discussion about different rules gives everybody the opportunity to express their point of view.

C ____________

Parents have to respect the rules too, and give a good example with their behaviour. You can't have a rule against bad language, for example, if a parent uses bad language.

D ____________

The family then discusses consequences and privileges. What happens if someone breaks the rules? Maybe they have to do more housework. Or maybe they can't go out at the weekend. Privileges, on the other hand, are rewards for respecting the rules. A typical privilege is having more time on the computer.

E ____________

The final step is to write down the rules, consequences and privileges. This is the contract. The family members then sign it and put it in a prominent place somewhere in the house.

3 Read again and correct the sentences.

1 Relationships between parents and teenagers are always difficult.
They are sometimes difficult.

2 Only Americans use family contracts.
____
____

3 Family contracts only cover homework and housework.
____
____

4 Parents can break the rules in the contract.
____
____

5 Nothing happens if teenagers respect the rules.
____
____

6 Only teenagers sign the contract.
____
____

2

ENGLISH YOU NEED

1 Match the underlined teen talk with the words below (standard English).

a Wait **c** are you ~~**e**~~ Yes
b doing **d** want to come **f** a lot

1 Sure. *e*
2 We've got loads of food. _
3 Hang on. _
4 What are you up to? _
5 How's it going? _
6 Do you fancy coming here? _

2 Complete the dialogue with the teen talk in exercise 1.

A Hi, Nick.
B Hi, Justin. (1) *How's it going?*
A Fine. (2) ______
B Nothing. Why?
A I'm with Simon at my house. (3) ______
B (4) ______
A You can eat here if you want. (5) ______
B OK. But my dad can't drive me home. Can I stay there?
A (6) ______ ... Yes, you can.
B Great! See you in about half an hour.

LISTENING

3 Circle your opinion.

In a family, it's best if ...

a only parents decide on house rules.
b parents and teenagers negotiate house rules.
c only teenagers decide on house rules.

4 3 Justin and Nick are talking. Listen and circle the correct option.

1 *Justin's parents / Justin and his parents* decided on their house rules.
2 Justin thinks his family contract is a *good / bad* idea.

5 3 Listen again. Answer the questions.

1 When did the family sign the contract?
About three months ago.
2 Is the contract very strict?
______
3 Does Nick's family have a contract?
______
4 What rule is there for Justin's father?
______
5 Who doesn't like the word 'wicked'?
______
6 What are the other rules about?
______

DICTATION

6 4 Listen. Write six sentences about Nick's family rules.

1 *Do* ______
2 ______
3 ______
4 ______
5 ______
6 ______

WRITING – An email

1 Do you think these rules are for school days (SD) or weekends (W)?

1 I can't go out. SD
2 I have to tidy my room. ___
3 I have to do my homework. ___
4 I can go out, but I mustn't get home late. ___
5 I don't have to do a lot of housework. ___
6 I have to do the ironing. ___

2 Read the email. Are the answers the same or different?

The same: 1, ________ Different: ________

> Hi!
> How are things? You asked about my house rules. Well, they're different for school days and weekends.
>
> On school days, I have to do homework and I can't go out. But I don't have to do a lot of housework. I make my bed, clear the table and help with the washing-up. That's all.
>
> But at weekends I have to tidy my room. I lay the table and I do the ironing.
>
> And I sometimes go to my grandparents' house to wash my grandad's car. I can go out but I mustn't get home late.
>
> I hope this answers your question.
>
> Dru

The apostrophe

3 Find examples of apostrophes in the email.

1 for a contraction: they're

________ ________

________ ________

2 for possession: ________

3 for possession after a word ending in *s*:

____

4 Write an apostrophe in each sentence.

1 I can go to stay at my best friends house.
friend's

2 Hes into music, like me. ________
3 We mustnt go to bed late. ________
4 But we can use his parents sound system.

____

5 We listen to all his dads CDs. ________
6 He doesnt have to ask permission. ________

5 Write about your rules.

On school days, I ________

____

____

At weekends, I ________

____

____

TRANSLATION

6 Translate the sentences.

1 I don't have to mop the floor.

____

2 My father has to do the washing-up.

____

____

3 You mustn't leave a mess when you go.

____

____

4 Do we have to go climbing?

____

5 Do you fancy going to the cinema?

____

____

6 I can't use my sister's computer.

____

SELF CHECK 2

Helping at home

1 Write the correct form of the verbs. _ / 5

mop do lay make take out

My family shares the housework. My mum (1) ________ the washing and the ironing. My dad (2) ________ the floor and we all (3) ____________ the rubbish. My sister (4) ________ the table and I clear it. And my sister and I always (5) ________ our beds.

Things I have to/don't have to do

2 Complete with the correct form of *have to*. _ / 5

A What's school like in the USA, Ethan?

B Well, in most states you (1) ____________ stay at school until you're 18, you can't leave at 16. Sports and other activities are important. You (2) ____________________ be in a school club, but most of us are.

A (3) ____________ you ____________ do exams?

B Yes, every school (4) ___________ set exams. But you (5) ____________________ pass a special one to go to university.

Permission and obligation

3 Write *can, can't/mustn't* or *don't have to* and a verb in the sentences about the UK. _ / 5

ride use learn make buy

1 You ______________ a motorbike without a helmet.

2 You ______________ a credit card to buy things in most shops.

3 You ____________________ schoolbooks. They're free!

4 You ______________ a copy of a CD. It's illegal.

5 You ______________ to drive when you're 17 in the UK, but not before.

Teen talk

4 Complete the conversation. _ / 5

A Hi, Jake. It's Miranda here. (1) H _ _' _ it g _ _ _ _ ?

B Fine, thanks, and you? (2) W _ _ _ are you _ _ _ _?

A Nothing special but I'm going to a concert in the park this afternoon. (3) L _ _ _ _ of people will be there. (4) D_ you f _ _ _ _ coming?

B (5) H _ _ _ _ _, I'll ask my mum if it's OK. ... Yes, it's fine. See you there.

Home rules

5 Circle the correct option. _ / 5

I live with my mum, my dad, my sister and my goldfish. My (1) *parents / parent's* aren't strict. I (2) *doesn't / don't* have to tidy my room and I can wear the clothes I like. I often wear my older (3) *sister's / sisters* clothes. I can't use my (4) *parent's / parents'* computer but I've got a laptop in my room. Oh, I have to look after our fish and change (5) *it's / its* water every week.

➟ **Answers** page 118

3 Reference TALKING CULTURE

GRAMMAR

Past simple

- See past simple forms on page 5.
- With regular verbs, we generally form the past simple by adding *-ed* to the infinitive.

Spelling rules

Most verbs	talk ask	+ *-ed*	talk**ed** ask**ed**
Verbs ending *-e*	dance live	+ *-d*	dance**d** live**d**
Verbs ending consonant + *-y*	identify verify	change *-y* to *-ied*	identif**ied** verif**ied**
Verbs ending consonant + vowel + consonant	shop travel	double consonant + *-ed*	shop**ped** travel**led**

- For irregular past simple verb forms, see the table on page 120.
- We use the past simple to talk about completed actions and situations in the past, often with a time expression such as *yesterday, last week,* etc.

They **walked** to school together **yesterday.**
Mr Grainger **didn't return** the book.
Where **did** everybody **go**?

1 Write the questions and answers.

1 **A** you / go / to the youth club / last night ?
Did you go to the youth club last night?

2 **B** no, / I / go / cinema

____

3 **A** What / you / see ?

____

4 **B** We / see / the latest Harry Potter film

____

5 **A** What / you / think / of it ?

____

6 **B** I / like / it / a lot

____

→ **Answers** page 116

there was/there were

Affirmative

- We use *there was/there were* to describe scenes in the past.

Affirmative
There was + a/an + singular countable noun There was + some + uncountable noun
There were + some + plural countable noun

There was a very tall man at the door.
There was some water on the floor.
There were four hotels in the square.

- Expressions of time or place go after the noun phrase.

There was some milk **in the fridge.**
NOT There was ~~in the fridge~~ some milk.

Negative

- In the negative, we generally use the contracted form *there wasn't* for singular countable nouns and uncountable nouns. We use *there weren't* for plural countable nouns.
- In the negative, we don't use *some*. We use *any* to express lack of something.

There wasn't any bread in the shop.
There weren't any internet cafés in those days.

Questions

- In questions, *was/were* appear at the beginning of the question.

Was there a big queue at the ticket office?

- We use *any* instead of *some*.
  Were there any Italians on the coach?

Short answers

Affirmative	Negative
Yes, there was. Yes, there were.	No, there wasn't. No, there weren't.

Was there any rice in the cupboard?
Yes, **there was**.

2 Complete the text with *there was* or *there wasn't* and there *were* or *there weren't*.

When I walked down the street, I noticed that (1) ___there were___ a lot of police officers around. (2) ______ a big crowd of people. (3) ______ any panic, though. Then I saw that (4) ______ a man lying on the ground. The police were pointing guns at him, and (5) ______ some fifty pound notes next to him. Unfortunately, (6) ______ any notes near me!

➟ **Answers** page 116

Adverbs

Spelling rules

Most adjectives	slow nervous beautiful	+ *-ly*	slowly nervously beautifully
Adjectives ending *-ble*	comfortable	change -e to *-y*	comfortably
Adjectives ending *-y*	happy angry	change *-y* to *-ily*	happily angrily
Irregular adjectives	good fast hard	irregular	well fast hard

- We use adverbs to describe the way something happens. They generally go after the main verb.
  'What are you doing?' he shouted **angrily**.

3 Make the adjectives into adverbs.

1 fast ___fast___
2 sad ______
3 confident ______
4 nervous ______
5 happy ______
6 slow ______

➟ **Answers** page 116

Past continuous

Affirmative
I was eating. You were eating. He was eating. She was eating. It was eating.
We were eating. You were eating. They were eating.

- We form the past continuous with the past simple of the verb *be* and the *–ing* form of the main verb.
  Frank and James **were playing** squash.
- See *-ing* spelling rules on page 8.

Negative	
Full form	Contracted form
I was not eating. You were not eating. He was not eating. She was not eating. It was not eating.	I wasn't eating. You weren't eating. He wasn't eating. She wasn't eating. It wasn't eating.
We were not eating. You were not eating. They were not eating.	We weren't eating. You weren't eating. They weren't eating.

Questions
Was I eating? Were you eating? Was he eating? Was she eating? Was it eating?
Were we eating? Were you eating? Were they eating?

Short answers	
Affirmative	**Negative**
Yes, I was. Yes, you were. Yes, he was. Yes, she was. Yes, it was.	No, I wasn't. No, you weren't. No, he wasn't. No, she wasn't. No, it wasn't.
Yes, we were. Yes, you were. Yes, they were.	No, we weren't. No, you weren't. No, they weren't.

- We use the past continuous to talk about something that was happening at a particular point in the past.
  At four o'clock yesterday afternoon I was flying over Paris.
- We can also use *wh-* questions with the past continuous.
  What game **were** the children **playing**?
- In short answers, we never repeat the *-ing* form.
  Were they watching the film?
  Yes, they **were**.
  NOT Yes, they were ~~watching~~.

4 Write the past continuous form of the verbs in brackets.

At seven o'clock yesterday evening ...

1 I *was mopping* (mop) the floors.
2 Gina ______________ (talk) about fashion.
3 we ______________________________ (study).
4 Mum and Dad ______________ (watch) TV.
5 my brother ______________ (chat) online.
6 it ______________________________ (not rain).

➞ **Answers** page 116

Past simple v. past continuous with *when/while*

Past simple	Past continuous
For complete actions in the past. Diana **stayed** with Karen for several weeks.	For actions that were in progress at a specific time in the past. Diana **was staying** with Karen last week.
After *when* in a past continuous sentence to introduce a second action. I was talking on the phone **when** you **arrived** home.	After *while* to describe two actions that were happening at the same time. I was talking on the phone **when/while** you **were cooking**.

5 Say the order in which the actions happened: first [1], second [2] or at the same time [S].

At seven o'clock yesterday evening ...

1 When I arrived home [S], my brother was listening to music and joking [S] with Tom.
2 They were telling jokes [_] while Georgia and I chatted [_] in the kitchen.
3 We were all talking very loudly [_] when there was a knock at the door [_].
4 When nobody answered the door, [_] the person knocked again [_].
5 We were all dancing [_] when the lights went out [_].
6 When a strange-looking man suddenly appeared at the back door [_] we got the shock of our lives [_].

➞ **Answers** page 116

VOCABULARY

Student's Multi-ROM Speaking dictionary

Adverbs

knock loudly	/nɒk 'laʊdli/	___
look suspiciously	/lʊk sə'spɪʃəsli/	___
ride carefully	/raɪd 'keəfəli/	___
sit calmly	/sɪt 'kɑːmli/	___
wait nervously	/weɪt 'nɜːvəsli/	___
walk slowly	/wɔːk 'sləʊli/	___

Types of art

drawing	/'drɔːɪŋ/	___
graffiti	/grə'fiːti/	___
painting	/'peɪntɪŋ/	___
photograph	/'fəʊtəgrɑːf/	___
portrait	/'pɔːtreɪt/	___
poster	/'pəʊstə/	___
sculpture	/'skʌlptʃə/	___
self-portrait	/self'pɔːtreɪt/	___

English you need

- Make and respond to suggestions

We could go to a museum.

___

That's a terrible idea.

___

Let's go shopping.

___

That's a good idea. How about going to Portobello Market?

___

You're joking.

___

Why don't we go on the London Eye?

___

Shall we meet later?

___

What about meeting back here at six o'clock?

___

Learning tip

- A good way to remember new words is to use them in a story.

1 Write these words in the story.

slowly self-portrait pavement worried ~~cockroach~~ landscape

Yesterday morning, I was walking to school when I saw a (1) *cockroach* on the (2) ___. I was walking (3) ___ because I was very (4) ___. When I arrived at school, I had an Art class. I drew a (5) ___. Next time I'll draw a (6) ___

2 Choose words from the word list in exercise 1 and write a story.

___

___

___

___

→ **Answers** page 116

3 TALKING CULTURE

VOCABULARY – Adverbs

1 Write the words in the sentences.

ful-re-ly-ca gri-an-ly ly-ful-be-ti-au ~~ow-ly-sl~~ iet-qu-ly ci-ly-spi-ous-su

① 

② 

③ 

④ 

⑤ 

⑥ 

1 He's driving very *slowly*

2 You paint ______

3 They're talking ______

4 She's choosing ______

5 He's acting very ______

6 He's looking ______ at the dog.

2 Write true sentences with a verb and an adverb.

1 *My mum sings badly.*

2 ______

3 ______

4 ______

5 ______

6 ______

GRAMMAR

Past simple

1 Write the past simple of the verbs.

not answer ~~be~~ pour not want strike echo

Paul (1) *was* nervous and he couldn't sleep. The clock in the hall (2) ____________ four o'clock and then five. Finally, at six o'clock, he got dressed and went to the kitchen. He (3) ____________ some milk and drank it. 'Are you OK?' his mother asked. Paul (4) ____________. He (5) ____________ to speak to anyone this morning. Instead, he took his school bag, and left the house. The street was empty and his footsteps (6) ____________ on the pavement. Ten minutes later, he stood in front of a big building. It was his first day at the new school.

2 Complete the questions.

1 *What time did Paul* get up?
He got up at six o'clock.

2 ____________ for breakfast?
He only had a glass of milk.

3 ____________
She asked 'Are you OK?'

4 ____________
He didn't say anything.

5 ____________ in the street?
He didn't see anyone.

6 ____________ nervous?
Because he was starting a new school.

there was/there were

3 Describe Paul's day. Use *there was* or *wasn't, there were* or *weren't* and *a, some* or *any*.

1 *There were some* students.
2 ____________ teacher.
3 ____________ posters?
4 No, ____________
5 ____________ piano.
6 ____________ drums.
7 ____________ music?
8 ____________

Adverbs

4 Change the adjectives to adverbs and write them in the story.

good careful happy ~~loud~~ nervous quick

At four o'clock that afternoon, Paul left the school with his new friends. They were all talking and laughing (1) *loudly*. Then he said goodbye and walked home, smiling (2) ________. He walked (3) ________ because he wanted to get home and tell his mum about his day. 'What was it like?', his mum asked him (4) ____________. 'It was great!', he said. He (5) ____________ explained all the details of his new school. And that night, he slept (6) ________

VOCABULARY – Types of art

1 Write the types of art.

1 photograph **3** ____-________ **5** _________

2 ________ **4** ______ **6** ________

2 Complete the sentences for you.

1 I've got a *photograph* of ______________________

2 I like a ____________ called ______________________

3 In my favourite ________________ there's ______________________

4 There's a ________________ of / by ________________ in my town/city.

GRAMMAR – Past continuous

3 Complete the description. Use the past continuous of the verbs.

live ~~stay~~ not feel not look walk rain

My favourite painting

Clara Duff

I saw this painting two years ago in New York. My family and I (**1**) *were staying* there with friends. One day, we (**2**) ____________ around the centre. It (**3**) ____________ so we visited a gallery. My parents aren't into art, so they (**4**) ____________________ very carefully at the paintings. Suddenly I saw *The Starry Night* by Vincent Van Gogh. He painted it in 1889, while he (**5**) ____________________ in France. It's very sad. Van Gogh was in hospital at the time, and he (**6**) ____________________ very happy.

4 Write questions in the past continuous.

A (1) *Were you walking your dog* at 8 o'clock last night?

B No, I wasn't.

A (2) ____________________?

B I was surfing the Internet.

A (3) ____________________

____

B No, I wasn't. I didn't have any homework last night.

A (4) ____________________?

B Jeans and a T-shirt, I think.

A (5) ____________________?

B I was feeling tired.

A (6) ____________________

____________________?

B My family? Mum and dad were watching TV and my sister was reading.

A Well, that's all for now. Thank you.

5 Answer the questions in exercise 2 for you.

1 *Yes, I was.*
2 ____________________
3 ____________________
4 ____________________

____
5 ____________________
6 ____________________

____

Past simple v. past continuous with *when*/*while*

6 Circle the correct option.

Spanish artist Pablo Picasso started to draw when he was very young. He (**1**) (*took*) / *was taking* art classes while he (**2**) *grew up* / *was growing up* in Malaga. In 1895 his family moved to Barcelona. He (**3**) *studied* / *was studying* art there when he (**4**) *had* / *was having* his first exhibition. That was in 1900. Over the next years Picasso made several trips to Paris. While he (**5**) *stayed* / *was staying* there, he (**6**) *met* / *was meeting* a lot of artists. He finally moved to Paris in 1904.

7 Write sentences in the past simple and continuous.

1 I / shop / the other day when I / see / an old friend

I was shopping the other day when

I saw an old friend.

2 He / not see / me because he / talk / on his mobile

____

____

3 I / notice / a crowd of people while I / go / home

____

____

4 The people / watch / a street artist

____

____

5 While he / draw / someone / put / some money in a hat

____

____

6 When / he / look up / to say thank you, I / recognise / my old friend

____

____

READING

1 Find the museum objects.

paintingssculpturesjewelleryphotographsdrawingsfurniture

1	*paintings*	**4**	______
2	______	**5**	______
3	______	**6**	______

2 Read the story and choose the best title.

a A strange encounter

b The broken necklace

c An old friend returns

3 Answer the questions.

1 Why was Laura in the museum?

She was on a school trip.

2 Why did she look at the necklace?

______

______

3 What happened while Laura was looking at the necklace?

______

______

4 What was the boy like?

______

______

5 What did he want to give Laura?

______

6 When did the boy disappear?

______

______

Last summer Laura went on a school trip to the Victoria and Albert Museum in London with her class. They were looking at some exhibits with their teacher when Laura saw a necklace. There was a lot of jewellery in the museum but the necklace was the most beautiful object. While she was looking at it, Laura suddenly felt very cold. Then she heard a strange voice behind her.

'Do you like it?'

She looked round and saw a boy. He was about the same age as her. His skin was very white and his clothes were black and old-fashioned.

'Yes, it's beautiful,' Laura said nervously.

The boy smiled coldly.

'Would you like it?'

Laura smiled. She looked around her. Her teacher was standing on the other side of the room, looking at her suspiciously.

'Why don't you put it on?'

'The necklace? You're joking. It's not mine.'

While she was speaking, she felt the boy's cold hands around her neck.

'You must wear the necklace!'

Suddenly another voice spoke.

'Laura? Are you all right?'

Her teacher was walking quickly across the room. She looked for the boy but he wasn't there.

ENGLISH YOU NEED

1 Match the parts of the suggestions and responses.

1	We could	**a**	terrible idea.
2	Shall we	**b**	looking at the paintings
3	How about	**c**	great.
4	Why don't	**d**	start with the sculptures.
5	That sounds	**e**	make a plan in the café?
6	That's a	**f**	we see the fashion collection?

2 Laura's talking to her friends. Write the sentences from exercise 1 in the dialogue.

Laura OK. Where shall we start?

Dean (1) *We could start with the sculptures.*

Ryan No way. I don't like sculpture.
(2) ______________________________?

Dean (3) ______________________________
Old clothes! I don't think so.

Laura (4) ______________________________?

Ryan OK, but there are a lot of rooms with paintings.

Laura (5) ______________________________?
Then we can have a drink too.

Maggie (6) ______________________________.
Let's do that.

LISTENING

3 5 Who was the boy in the story? Can you guess? Listen and check.

______________________________.

4 5 Listen again. Are the sentences true or false? Correct the false sentences.

1 Laura's teacher believes her.
False – he thinks she was dreaming.

2 The Prince gave the necklace to a princess.
____

3 The princess loved the prince.
____

4 He killed her while he was putting the necklace around her neck.
____

5 They see a photo of the prince in the gallery.
____

6 The prince died a long time ago.
____

DICTATION

5 6 Listen. Write six sentences from the story.

1 *Laura* ______________________________

2 ______________________________

3 ______________________________

4 ______________________________

5 ______________________________

6 ______________________________

WRITING – A story

1 Put the events in the story in order.

_ It was Brad Pitt.
1 We were celebrating my mum's birthday.
_ I asked for an autograph.
_ Someone sat at the table behind us.

Time connectors

2 Complete the story with the time connectors. Was your order correct?

at first   a few minutes later
then   ~~when~~   eventually

Something amazing happened (1) *when* we went to a restaurant to celebrate my mum's birthday. We finished our meal, and then they brought a cake and we sang happy birthday.
(2) __________, someone sat at the table behind us. It was Brad Pitt.
(3) __________, I couldn't believe it, but (4) __________ I looked around me. Everyone was looking too.
My mum likes Brad Pitt, so (5) __________ I asked for an autograph. 'Could you sign my mum's birthday card?' I asked nervously. 'Sure', he said, and signed his name.

3 Answer the questions and complete a story.

1 What were you doing? Who did you see?
One day my friends and I were __________
when __________

2 What were your first reactions? How did they change?
At first __________
but then __________

3 What happened next?
A few minutes later __________

4 How did the story end?
Eventually, __________

CORRECTION

4 Correct the sentences.

1 While we walked home, we met a friend. ✗
While we were walking home, we met a friend.

2 He was acting suspicious. ✗

3 There wasn't any other people outside. ✗

4 When we were seeing him, he was painting graffiti on a wall. ✗

5 How about go for a drink with me? ✗

6 That's terrible idea. ✗

How people do things

1 Change the adjective to an adverb and write in the sentences. _ / 5

angry careful good loud patient

1 His neighbours didn't hear the doorbell so he knocked ________ on the door.
2 I want to learn to speak English ________
3 'You're late again!' the teacher said ________
4 Kate took off her shoes and put them ________ back in the box.
5 The bus was late, but we waited ________ for it to arrive.

A scene in the past

2 Complete with the correct form of *there was* or *were* and *there wasn't* or *weren't*. _ / 5

A What did you see when you opened the door?
B We saw a desk with some books on it. (1) ________ ________ a light in the corner of the room, but (2) ________ ________ any windows.
A (3) ________ ________ any bottles in the room?
B Yes, (4) ________ ________. But (5) ________ ________ anything in the bottles, they were all empty. Then …

The story of a picture

3 Write the verbs in the past simple or continuous. _ / 5

Van Gogh (1) ________ (paint) his famous picture *Sunflowers* while he (2) ________ (live) in the south of France. He (3) ________ (rent) a house in Arles at the time, and he and the French painter Paul Gauguin (4) ________ (use) it as a studio. He (5) ________ (want) to decorate the house so he produced four paintings of sunflowers.

Suggestions

4 Write the phrases in the dialogue. _ / 5

How about That sounds great. Why don't we shall we That's a terrible idea.

A What (1) ________ do this weekend?
B I don't know. (2) ________ stay at home and watch TV?
A (3) ________ Let's go to a museum or an art gallery for a change.
B OK. (4) ________ going to the new exhibition at the National Gallery?
A (5) ________ I really want to learn more about art.

A story

5 Circle the correct option. _ / 5

One afternoon, I was walking home from school (1) *when / while* I saw a crowd of people in the street. (2) *At first / At the beginning*, I continued walking. Then two men ran out of the crowd. They were wearing masks. 'They're robbers', I thought and I ran after them. A few seconds (3) *after / later*, someone in the crowd shouted, 'Cut!' They (4) *made / were making* a film. I was very embarrassed but (5) *at the end / eventually*, we all laughed about it and I stayed and watched them film the scene again.

➡ **Answers** page 118

4 Reference

ATTITUDES

GRAMMAR

too much, *too many*, *not enough*

- We use *too much* and *too many* to say that we have got more than we need of something.
- We use *not enough* to say that we need more of something.
- We can use these expressions with *there is/there are* and *have got*:

too much + uncountable noun	We've got **too much food** here. We'll never eat it all.
too many + plural countable noun	There are **too many people**. We need more chairs.

not enough + uncountable noun	We haven**'t** got **enough time** to wrap the presents now. We'll do it later.
not enough + plural countable noun	There aren**'t enough cars**. Some people will have to walk.

1 Complete the dialogue with *too much*, *too many* and *enough*.

A The recipe says we need five aubergines, but I only have one. I haven't got (1) ___*enough*___ aubergines.

B But that recipe is for six people. There are only two of us. We'll have (2) ______________ food.

A Maybe the problem is that there aren't (3) ______________ people. I'll invite Jack and Jane, and maybe Dave. Anyway, there's a special offer on aubergines at the market. I don't mind having (4) ______________ aubergines. We can use them for something else.

B OK, but you'd better go to the market now, or there won't be (5) ______________ time to make the recipe. And don't start inviting (6) ______________ people!

➟ **Answers** page 116

Quantifiers

- There are several quantifiers we can use before countable and uncountable nouns. These include: *a lot of*, *a little*, *a few*, *some*, (*not*) *any*.
- We can use (*not*) *any*, *some* and *a lot of* with both uncountable nouns and plural countable nouns.
  I have**n't** got **any milk**.
  There are**n't any biscuits**.
  We've got **some information**.
  There are **some German students** over there.
  There's **a lot of noise** outside.
  You've got **a lot of friends**.
- However, we only use *a few* with plural countable nouns and *a little* with uncountable nouns.
  There were **a few boys** in the playground.
  I only need to borrow **a little money**.
- We use *How much?* and *How many?* to ask about quantity.

How much + uncountable nouns
How much chocolate do you eat in a week?

How many + plural countable nouns
How many brothers and sisters have you got?

2 Circle the correct word.

A What do you spend your pocket money on?
B Lots of things, but mainly CDs.
A How (**1**) *much* / *many* have you got?
B About 75.
A Wow! That's (**2**) *a few* / *a lot of* CDs.
B I've got (**3**) *some* / *any* DVDs as well, but I've only got (**4**) *a little* / *a few* of them.
A I haven't got (**5**) *some* / *any* time to listen to music or watch films these days. There's always homework to do.
B We're lucky. At our school, we only get (**6**) *a few* / *a little* homework.

➡ **Answers** page 116

4 Reference

VOCABULARY

Student's Multi-ROM Speaking dictionary

City life

adverts	/ˈædvɜːts/	___
buildings	/ˈbɪldɪŋs/	___
crowds	/kraʊds/	___
cycle lanes	/ˈsaɪkl leɪns/	___
green spaces	/griːn ˈspeɪsɪz/	___
litter	/ˈlɪtə/	___
parking metres	/ˈpɑːkɪŋ ˈmiːtəs/	___
pollution	/pəˈluːʃn/	___
recycling bins	/riːˈsaɪklɪŋ bɪns/	___
satellite dishes	/ˈsætəlaɪt ˈdɪʃɪz/	___
solar panels	/ˈsəʊlə ˈpænəlz/	___
traffic	/ˈtræfɪk/	___

Adjectives for emotions

annoyed	/əˈnɔɪd/	___
annoying	/əˈnɔɪɪŋ/	___
bored	/bɔːd/	___
boring	/ˈbɔːrɪŋ/	___
confused	/kənˈfjuːzd/	___
confusing	/kənˈfjuːzɪŋ/	___
excited	/ɪkˈsaɪtɪd/	___
exciting	/ɪkˈsaɪtɪŋ/	___
frightened	/ˈfraɪtnd/	___
frightening	/ˈfraɪtnɪŋ/	___
relaxed	/rɪˈlækst/	___
relaxing	/rɪˈlæksɪŋ/	___

English you need

- React strongly

How terrifying!

___

They're really fascinating.

___

What a terrible CD!

___

They're very friendly.

___

They look absolutely disgusting.

___

It's really exciting.

___

Learning tip

- Idioms are a type of expression. You can't predict their meaning from the individual words, so it's important to note their meaning.

1 Choose the meaning of the underlined idiom.

1 - a

1 Sally and James are both vegetarians now. They're birds of a feather, those two.
a people with the same ideas and interests
b people with an interest in birds

2 My brother always plays terrible music. It drives me mad.
a It's really exciting.
b It's really annoying.

3 I know that I passed the exam. It was a piece of cake!
a very difficult
b very easy

4 I'm not going out tonight. I feel under the weather. I've got a headache and a cold.
a cold
b ill

5 My mum's got a fantastic new job. She's over the moon.
a really happy
b disappointed

2 Choose two idioms from exercise 1 and write a true sentence for each one.

1 ______________________________

____

2 ______________________________

____

→ **Answers** page 116

4 ATTITUDES

VOCABULARY City life

1 Do the puzzle.

cycle lanes litter traffic ~~adverts~~ buildings green spaces pollution
solar panels crowds parking meters satellite dishes recycling bins

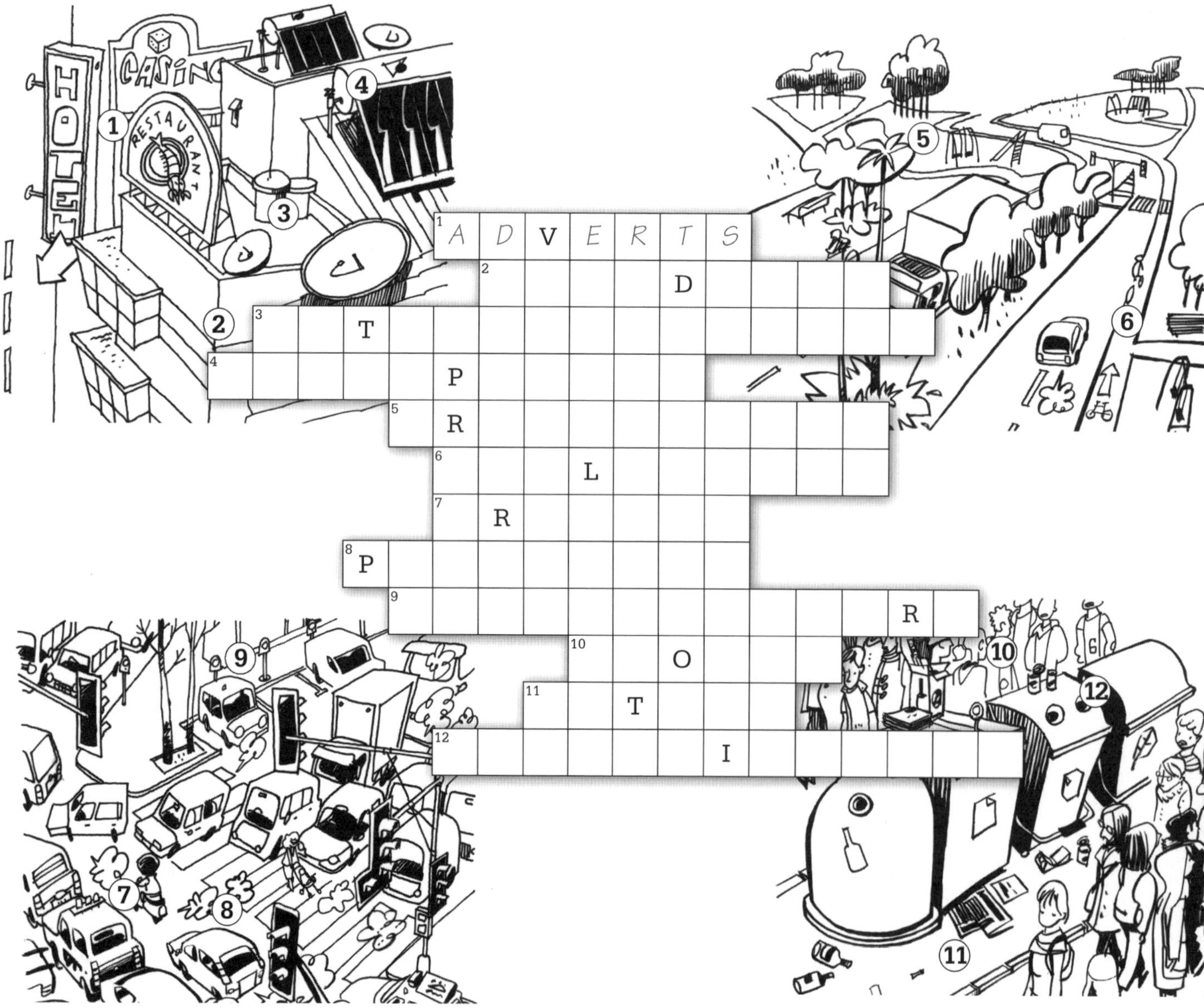

2 What can you see when you look out of the window in your home?

I can see some ______________________________

I can also see ______________________________

I can't see ______________________________

GRAMMAR *too much, too many, not enough*

1 Complete the sentences with *there is* or *there are* and *too much* or *too many*.

1 *There's too much* traffic.
2 ______________ people.
3 ______________ adverts.
4 ______________ rubbish.
5 ______________ bikes.
6 ______________ graffiti.

2 Write sentences with *not enough*.

Let's take action for a better world!

In many parts of the world …

1 there / be / schools
2 people / have got / water
3 there / be / food
4 hospitals / have got / doctors
5 there / be / medicines
6 workers / make / money

1 *There aren't enough schools.*
2 ______________
3 ______________
4 ______________
5 ______________
6 ______________

3 Complete the letter with *be* or *have got* and *too much, too many* or *not enough*.

Dear Sir / Madam,

I'm writing because we need to take action in our city. There (1) *are too many cars* (cars) and there (2) ______________ (pollution). There (3) ______________ (cycle lanes) and we (4) ______________ (green spaces). There (5) ______________ (litter) on our streets too, and that's because we (6) ______________ (bins) to put our rubbish in. What is the government going to do about these things?

Yours sincerely,

Stan Gemmel

4 Write six sentences about you and your town / city. Use *too much, too many* and *not enough*.

1 *There aren't enough places to go out at night.*
2 ______________
3 ______________
4 ______________
5 ______________
6 ______________

VOCABULARY Adjectives for emotions

1 Write the adjectives.

1 ~~aoynend~~ 3 funcdose 5 rihtdfenge
2 rxlaede 4 teciedx 6 oebdr

1 *annoyed* 4 ______
2 ______ 5 ______
3 ______ 6 ______

2 Write the adjectives from exercise 1 with *-ing*. What does each adjective describe for you?

1 *annoying – when I can't find my keys*
2 ______
3 ______
4 ______
5 ______
6 ______

3 Write an adjective with *-ed* or *-ing*.

disappoint disgust tire ~~interest~~
surprise embarrass

1 I love watching documentaries about animals. They're really *interesting*
2 My friend was ______ when she forgot my birthday.
3 I went to bed early last night because I was ______
4 Although it was an expensive restaurant, the meal was ______
5 We were ______ when we saw our photo in a magazine.
6 I think cruelty to animals is ______

GRAMMAR Quantifiers

4 Read about Jamie's hobbies. Write sentences with *a lot of*, *some* and *not any*.

I love sports. I play basketball, football, volleyball and tennis. I like TV programmes like the news and documentaries but I don't like reality shows or quiz shows. And I never watch soap operas – they're boring!
I'm into different types of music, especially rock, dance, hip hop and reggae but I never buy classical CDs.
I listen to Kayne West and Jay-Z but I don't like all rap singers.

1 play / sport

He plays a lot of sports.

2 like / TV programmes

3 not watch / soap operas

4 be into / types of music

5 not buy / classical CDs

6 listen to / rap artists

5 Circle the correct option. Are the sentences the same for you? Tick (✓) or cross (✗).

1 Jamie spends (*a little*) / *a few* time every evening on his computer.

2 He keeps *a little* / *a few* comics and magazines, but not many.

3 He spends *a little* / *a few* money on going out, but not much.

4 He prefers to have *a little* / *a few* good friends than a lot of friends.

5 He usually does *a little* / *a few* homework before dinner.

6 He sees *a little* / *a few* DVDs every month.

1 ✓ 3 _ 5 _

2 _ 4 _ 6 _

4

6 Write questions in the survey. Use *How much?* or *How many?* Then circle your answer.

Class Survey

1 books you / read a year ?

a 10+ **b** 1–10 **c** 0

2 time / you / spend watching TV every day ?

a 2+ hours **b** 1–2 hours **c** less than 1 hour

3 money / you / spend on clothes every week ?

a 10+ euros **b** 5–10 euros **c** 0–5 euros

4 sports / you / play ?

a 3+ **b** 1–2 **c** 0

5 pocket money / you / get ?

a 10+ euros **b** 5–10 euros **c** 0–5 euros

6 films / you / see at the cinema every year ?

a 15+ **b** 5–15 **c** less than 5

7 Write your results from the survey. Use *a lot of*, *some*, *not any*, *a little* and *a few*.

1 *I read a few books every year.*

2

3

4

5

6

READING

1 Which of these things are you frightened of? Tick (✓) them.

1 spiders	☐	**3** flying	☐	**5** crowds of people	☐
2 rats	☐	**4** storms	☐	**6** speaking in public	☐

2 Read on the Internet postings about phobias. Match them (A–D) with the pictures.

A 2 **B** _ **C** _ **D** _

1 

2 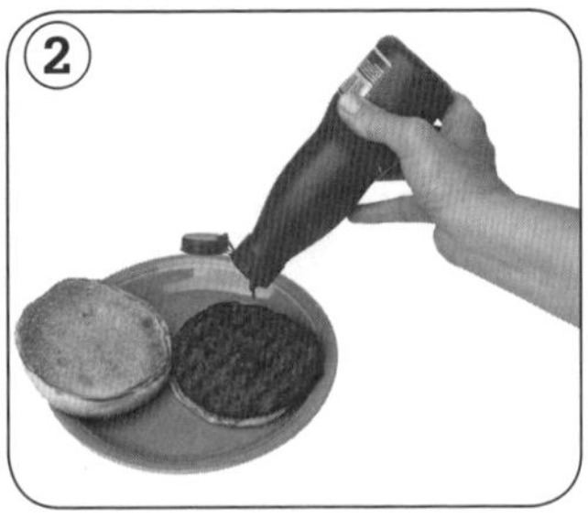

3 

4 

We all know people with a fear of spiders or heights. But the list of possible phobias is endless. In fact, if you think your phobia is unusual, think again. Someone else finds it scary too!

Here are some postings from our Internet forum.

A My brother's absolutely terrified of ketchup. If any ketchup comes near him, he runs away. He says the smell is the worst thing. The problem is that people think he's joking. Is anyone else frightened of ketchup?

B My best friend has a fear of putting her clothes on the wrong way round. She's always checking to see if the label of her jumper is at the back. Is there a name for this fear?

C I'm frightened of buttons, especially plastic buttons. I can't wear shirts with buttons on, and for me, touching a button is like touching a spider. People don't believe me, so it's good to see I'm not alone!

D I'm scared of y*ll*w c*rs. I can't write the words! One day one parked in front of my house, and I couldn't go to school. I hate them! They're bright on the outside, but really dark inside.

3 Write the posting or postings.

1 The posting's about somebody else's phobia. A, ______
2 The writer doesn't like writing the name of the phobia. ______
3 The writer wants to know the name of the phobia. ______
4 People don't think this is really a phobia. ______, ______
5 The writer couldn't leave home one day. ______
6 The phobia's connected to clothes. ______, ______

ENGLISH YOU NEED

1 Match the underlined adjectives with the extreme adjectives.

amazing ~~delicious~~ disgusting
fascinating terrifying terrible

1 This fish is nice. *delicious*
2 Spiders are frightening. ______
3 This film's bad. ______
4 Those paintings are good. ______
5 Maths is interesting. ______
6 This pasta's not nice. ______

2 Complete the dialogues with the words below. You can use words twice.

absolutely how very ~~what~~

A (1) *What* an amazing poster!
B Do you like it? I think it's (2) ______ terrible.

A Tony, you put ketchup on your salad. (3) ______ disgusting!
B It's (4) ______ nice. Try some!

A *1984*! (5) ______ a great book!
B Yes. It's (6) ______ fascinating.

LISTENING

3 7 Choose the correct options. Then listen to Olivia and check your answers.

1 George Orwell was …
a a writer b a film director
2 One of his works is called …
a *Big Brother* b *1984*
3 The main character has a fear of …
a cameras b rats

4 7 Listen again and circle the correct option about the book *1984*.

1 It's about life in (*the future*) / *another world*.
2 People *are* / *aren't* free.
3 Big Brother's a *country* / *government*.
4 There are *cameras* / *people* everywhere.
5 In Room 101, everybody sees *rats* / *their worst fear*.
6 Olivia thinks the book's *bad* / *exciting*.

DICTATION

5 8 Listen. Write six sentences about Olivia.

1 *I've got* ______
2 ______
3 ______
4 ______
5 ______
6 ______

WRITING — My loves and hates

1 Do you like these things?

1 music _		**4** politics _	
2 adventure sports _		**5** nature _	
3 poetry _		**6** celebrities _	

2 Read the message from a website. How many likes and dislikes do you share?

> What's up? I'm Jay, a guy from Bristol – with attitude! I'm into adventure sports because they're exciting. But I like listening to music and reading poetry too.
>
> I'm also interested in politics and I've got a lot of opinions! I hate the fact that some people are rich when other people haven't got enough to eat – it's disgusting! I love nature and I hate pollution. I think there are too many programmes about celebrities on TV. They drive me mad!
>
> If you share my opinions – or if you don't – write to me. Let's talk!

Referencing

3 What do the underlined words refer to? Draw an arrow and circle the words.

1 I'm Jay. If you share my opinions – or if you don't – write to me.

2 I love adventure sports. They're exciting.

3 My favourite poet is Bob Dylan. I love his poetry.

4 Nature is important. We need to protect it.

5 We're destroying the environment. Why are we doing this?

6 There are too many programmes about celebrities. They drive me mad.

4 Write your response to Jay. Complete the sentences.

Hi Jay!

I'm ____________ and I'm from ____________

____________. I'm into____________

because ____________

I like____________ too.

I love ____________

I hate ____________

I also think ____________

I don't think ____________

TRANSLATION

5 Translate the sentences.

1 There's too much rubbish in the streets.

____

____

2 We've got a few green spaces.

____

____

3 There aren't enough cycle lanes.

____

____

4 It's annoying when people arrive late.

____

____

5 What a disgusting spider!

____

____

6 How many people are afraid of insects?

____

____

SELF CHECK 4

Things in a city

1 Complete the advert. _ / 5

Come to Newtown!

Newtown is a new kind of town. There are no cars in the town centre, and because there isn't any (**1**) t ________, there isn't any (**2**) p ________ here - the air is clean and fresh. People only travel by bicycle and there are (**3**) c ________ l ________ in every area. Nobody is more than two minutes from (**4**) r ________ b ________ for their rubbish, and most buildings have (**5**) s ________ p ________ on the top to produce electricity.

Problems

2 Complete with the verbs and with *too much*, *too many* or *not enough*. _ / 5

'Hi, this is a message for Ronan. Sorry, I can't come to your party.
I (1) ________________ (have got) homework at the moment, and there (2) ________________ (be) tests at school. I've got music exams too, but I (3) ________________ (have got) time to practise for them. And it's difficult to concentrate in this house. There (4) ________________ (be) quiet moments in the day because my sisters (5) ________________ (make) noise!
Anyway, have a good party.'

Quantities

3 Circle the correct option. _ / 5

A How (1) *much* / *many* food have we got?
B Let me see. We've got (2) *a little* / *a few* bread.
A How (3) *much* / *many* tomatoes are there?
B We've got (4) *a little* / *a few* tomatoes.
A What about pasta?
B No, we haven't got (5) *some* / *any* pasta.
A OK. Let's phone for a pizza!

Strong reactions

4 Complete the dialogue with the words. _ / 5

delicious an amazing disgusting good terrifying

A What (1) ________________ horror film! I was very frightened.
B Me too. It was absolutely (2) ________________
A The special effects were very (3) ________________ too.
B Right. Do you remember when the man eats a spider?
A How (4) ________________ ! I hate spiders.
B But did you see the man's face? He thought it was (5) ________________

My loves and hates

5 Circle the correct option. _ / 5

Hi Ian!
Thanks for your email. I think hip-hop and dance music are really (1) … too. I often listen to (2) … on my MP3 player. But I'm not (3) … in politics. My best friend talks about politics all day, and I can't stand (4) … I think it's (5) … Right now I prefer to think about music.

1 a excited b exciting
2 a it b them
3 a interested b interesting
4 a it b him
5 a bored b boring

➡ **Answers** page 118

EXPERIENCES

GRAMMAR

Present perfect

Affirmative	
Full form	**Contracted form**
I have worked. You have worked. He has worked. She has worked. It has worked.	I've worked. You've worked. He's worked. She's worked. It's worked.
We have worked. You have worked. They have worked.	We've worked. You've worked. They've worked.

Negative	
Full form	**Contracted form**
I have not worked. You have not worked. He has not worked. She has not worked. It has not worked.	I haven't worked. You haven't worked. He hasn't worked. She hasn't worked. It hasn't worked.
We have not worked. You have not worked. They have not worked.	We haven't worked. You haven't worked. They haven't worked.

- We form the present perfect with the verb *have* and the past participle.
- The past participle of regular verbs ends in *-ed*. It has the same form as the past simple ending. See the past simple spelling rules on page 32.
  Past simple: John **lived** in China.
  Present perfect: John **has lived** in China.
- The past participle forms of irregular verbs need to be learnt individually. See page 120.
- We use the present perfect to talk about experiences that happened at any time in the past. We don't have to use a time expression to say when the event happened.
  Linda**'s won** another prize.
- However, it can appear with an incomplete time expression such as *today, this week, this month, recently*, etc.
  I've made so many mistakes **this morning**. (It is still morning.)

been v. *gone*

- The verb *go* has two past participle forms: *been* and *gone*.
- We use *been* when we know that someone has returned from a journey. We use *gone* when they have not returned.
  Josh **has been** to India. (He is back now.)
  Josh **has gone** to India. (He is still in India.)

1 Look at the table and complete the sentences.

	go to lots of concerts	travel to different countries	meet interesting people
Lydia	✓	✗	✓
Ryan	✗	✓	✓
Scott	✓	✗	✗

During the past year …

1 Lydia *has been* to lots of concerts.
2 Ryan ______________ to lots of concerts.
3 Lydia and Scott ______________ to different countries.
4 Ryan ______________ to different countries.
5 Lydia and Ryan ______________ interesting people.
6 Scott ______________ interesting people.

➡ **Answers** page 116

Present perfect: questions

Questions
Have I worked? Have you worked? Has he worked? Has she worked? Has it worked?
Have we worked? Have you worked? Have they worked?

Short answers	
Affirmative	Negative
Yes, I have. Yes, you have. Yes, he has. Yes, she has. Yes, it has.	No, I haven't. No, you haven't. No, he hasn't. No, she hasn't. No, it hasn't.
Yes, we have. Yes, you have. Yes, they have.	No, we haven't. No, you haven't. No, they haven't.

- We use question words to make *wh-* questions.
  What other countries **have** you **visited**?
- In questions, we often use *ever*, which means *at any time in your life*. We put *ever* just before the past participle.
  Has this **ever happened** before?
- In short answers, we repeat the auxiliary *have/has* rather than the past participle.
  Have you **seen** the new James Bond film?
  Yes, I **have**.
  NOT Yes, ~~I've seen.~~

2 Write the questions.

1 Jane / ever / cook / a meal / for her family ?
Has Jane ever cooked a meal for her family?

2 you / go / to / the USA ?
____

3 Where / Matt and Fiona / move to ?
____

4 How often / you / swim / in the Mediterranean ?
____

5 your parents / buy / a new car ?
____

6 you / ever / see / a ghost ?
____

➡ **Answers** page 116

just

- We use *just* with the present perfect affirmative or interrogative to talk about something that happened a very short time ago.
- The word *just* goes immediately before the past participle.
  They**'ve just arrived**.
  Has he **just finished**?

3 Write the sentences with *just*.

1 Have they arrived?
Have they just arrived?

2 Peter's left for school.
____

3 I've seen Mary and Tony.
____

4 They've been on holiday.
____

5 Has Alex invited you to his party?
____

6 Have you had a shower?
____

➡ **Answers** page 116

VOCABULARY

Student's Multi-ROM Speaking dictionary

Jobs

architect	/'ɑːkɪtekt/	________
chef	/ʃef/	________
computer programmer	/kəm'pjuːtə 'prəʊgræmə/	________
engineer	/endʒɪ'nɪə/	________
hairdresser	/'heədresə/	________
journalist	/'dʒɜːnəlɪst/	________
lawyer	/'lɔjə/	________
mechanic	/mə'kænɪk/	________
shop assistant	/ʃɒp ə'sɪstənt/	________
social worker	/'səʊʃl 'wɜːkə/	________
vet	/vet/	________
waiter	/'weɪtə/	________

Life experiences

come home	/kʌm həʊm/	________
eat snails	/iːt 'sneɪlz/	________
go on a rollercoaster	/gəʊ ɒn ə 'rəʊləkəʊstə/	________
send someone a Valentine's card	/send 'sʌmwn ə 'vælentaɪnz kɑːd/	________
sing a song	/sɪŋ ə sɒŋ/	________
speak to a famous person	/spiːk tu ə 'feɪməs 'pɜːsən/	________
win a prize	/wɪn ə praɪz/	________
write a poem	/raɪt ə 'pəʊɪm/	________

English you need

- Join a club

Can you give me some information, please?

____

How old do you have to be to join?

____

What does membership include?

____

Do I get anything else?

____

You get two free passes.

____

How much does it cost to join?

____

You have to complete this membership form.

____

Learning tip

- Writing words in different categories helps you to remember them.

1 Write two jobs in these categories.

1 well-paid (with a high salary)
engineer ______________ ______________

2 badly-paid (with a low salary)
______________ ______________

3 in a restaurant
______________ ______________

4 in an office
______________ ______________

5 with the public
______________ ______________

6 in a uniform
______________ ______________

2 Write one life experience in these categories.

1 something exciting
____

2 something romantic
____

3 something horrible
____

4 something creative
____

5 something frightening
____

6 something unusual
____

➟ **Answers** page 116

5 EXPERIENCES

VOCABULARY Jobs

1 Complete the crossword.

Across

4 This person designs buildings. (9)
6 An important cook in a restaurant. (4)
7 This person writes articles for newspapers. (10)
9 A doctor for animals. (3)
10 You order food from this person in a restaurant. (6)
11 A designer of software programs for computers. (8, 10)
12 This person uses Maths and Science to construct new things. (8)

Down

1 This person helps people with problems. (6, 6)
2 You go to this person for a haircut. (11)
3 This person can repair your car or motorbike. (8)
5 This person serves you in a shop. (4, 9)
8 You go to this person if you have legal questions. (6)

2 Write two jobs you'd like and two you wouldn't like.

1 I'd like to be a ______________ because ______________________________
2 I'd also like to be a ______________ because ______________________________
3 I don't want to be a ______________ because ______________________________
4 I don't want to be a ______________ because ______________________________

GRAMMAR

Present perfect

1 Write the past participles next to the infinitives.

1 read *read*
2 see ______
3 have ______
4 forget ______
5 make ______
6 sell ______
7 forgive ______
8 meet ______

2 Write about Emma's and Charlie's experiences. Use verbs from exercise 1.

	Emma	Charlie
a lot of books	✓	✗
a famous person	✓	✓
a ghost	✓	✗
a bad dream	✓	✗
a cake	✓	✓
a friend's birthday	✗	✓

1 Emma *'s read a lot of books.*
2 Emma and Charlie ______
3 Charlie ______
4 Emma ______
5 Emma and Charlie ______
6 Charlie ______

been v. *gone*

3 Match a sentence with a response.

1 *b* 2 _ 3 _ 4 _ 5 _ 6 _

1 Your sister's very brown.
2 Where's your sister?
3 Aren't your parents at home?
4 Have we got any milk?
5 Does Paul know London well?
6 Is Paul in London?

a Yes, he's been there three times.
b She's been to Majorca on holiday.
c No, they've gone shopping.
d Yes, he's gone there for the weekend.
e Yes, mum and dad have been shopping.
f She's gone to Majorca with her friends.

4 Read the information about Paula's grandad and write sentences in the present perfect.

'My grandad's had an interesting life. He was born in Canada, but he came to England when he was sixteen. His first job was as a mechanic, and then he became a teacher. When he retired, he wrote a novel. And it's a bestseller! Now he's 70, but he still has ambitions. He tried salsa dancing recently and now he's learning to play a musical instrument.
This summer, we all went to Canada to meet my cousins for the first time.'

1 Paula's grandad *'s lived in two* countries.
2 He ______ the same job all his life.
3 He ______ a book.
4 A lot of people ______ it.
5 He ______ salsa dancing.
6 He and his family ______ to Canada.

VOCABULARY – Life experiences

1 Match the parts of the phrases.

8 things to do when you're young!

1
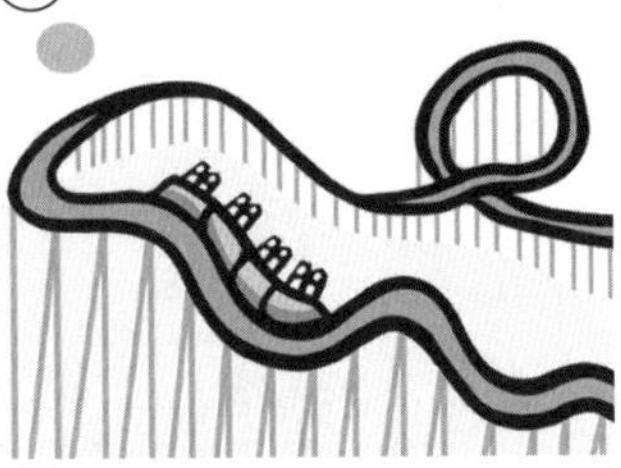

5

2

6

3

7

4

8

1	Go	**a**	to a famous person.
2	Get	**b**	a poem.
3	Sing	**c**	home after midnight.
4	Eat	**d**	a prize in a competition.
5	Win	**e**	someone a Valentine's card.
6	Write	**f**	a song in public.
7	Speak	**g**	snails.
8	Send	**h**	on a rollercoaster

2 Write about your experiences.

✓ *I've been on a roller coaster, I've* __________

____

✗ *I haven't* __________

____

GRAMMAR

Present perfect: questions

3 Write questions. Then answer them.

1 scientists / clone / animals ?
Have scientists cloned animals?
Yes, they have.

2 Russian astronauts / walk / on the Moon ?
____
____
____

3 Madrid / hold / the Olympic Games ?
____
____
____

4 George Clooney / win / an Oscar ?
____
____
____

5 France / have / a woman president ?
____
____
____

6 tourists / travel / in space ?
____
____
____

4 Complete the questions. Then answer the questions for you.

A Let me try this culture questionnaire. What (1) *museums have you visited* ?

B I've only visited the Science Museum.

A How many (2) __________ ?

B I've been to the theatre three or four times.

A Which (3) __________ ?

B I haven't read any Harry Potter books.

A What (4) ______________________________
______________________________?

B I haven't heard many classical composers. Just Mozart.

A How many (5) ______________________________
______________________________?

B I've watched at least three Spielberg films.

A Who (6) ______________________________
______________________________?

B I've seen Coldplay in concert.

1 *I've visited* ______________________________
2 ______________________________
3 ______________________________
4 ______________________________
5 ______________________________
6 ______________________________

5 Complete the questionnaire. Use *ever*.

1 ~~you~~ 2 a document
3 you 4 a stranger
5 you 6 a friend

disappear find
~~arrive~~ leave finish
forget

How disorganised are you?

1 *Have you ever arrived* late for an exam?

2 ______________________________ from your computer?

3 ______________________________ your keys in the front door?

4 ______________________________ your wallet or purse in the street?

5 ______________________________ a friend's birthday?

6 ______________________________ the credit on your mobile?

5

6 Write your answers to the questionnaire. Use *never* if necessary.

I've never arrived late for an exam.
____
____
____
____
____

just

7 Write a second sentence with *just* and the words below.

finish school wake up arrive
~~have lunch~~ leave start to rain

1 I'm not hungry now.
I've just had lunch.

2 John and Jessie aren't here.
____

3 Lucy's really happy.
____

4 Have you got an umbrella?
____

5 I feel really sleepy.
____

6 Have your ever read this letter?
____

8 Write about what has just happened in your life. Use the verbs below or others.

finish watch phone listen to have speak to

I've just finished
____
____
____
____
____
____
____

READING

1 Can you name three famous theme parks? Where are they?

1 *Universal Studios, USA* 2 ______ 3 ______

2 Match the adverts and the pictures.

1 ______ 2 *Disneyland, Paris* 3 ______

The United States has got more theme parks than any other country in the world. But there are some amazing theme parks in Europe too. Here are some of the best.

Efteling, Holland

Opened in the 1930s, Efteling was an inspiration for Walt Disney. Today it's a magical forest, full of medieval dragons and ogres. Here, you can meet your favourite storybook characters and enjoy a ride on the double-loop rollercoaster Python. And don't miss the 3-D film Panda Vision; the animals throw fruit at you and splash you with water.

PortAventura, Spain

Have you ever travelled to Mexico and China on the same day? You can here. PortAventura opened in 1995, and has five zones, each with its own shows and rides. The Dragon Khan is the biggest rollercoaster, but you can also experience sea monsters in the futuristic Sea Odyssey, and a 110kph fall from the Hurakan Condor tower.

Disneyland, Paris

One of Europe's most popular theme parks, Disneyland Paris opened in 1992. It has four lands: Frontierland, with its cowboys; Adventureland, with Caribbean islands; Fantasyland, with the Sleeping Beauty Castle, and Discoveryland, with the amazing Space Mountain, Mission 2 ride. For many, The Pirates of the Caribbean ride here is the best in the world.

3 Write the name of the theme park, D (Disneyland), P (PortAventura) or E (Efteling).

1 *E* is the oldest of the three parks.
2 _ and _ have areas representing different countries.
3 You walk through trees at _
4 You go down very fast on one of the rides at _
5 There are futuristic rides at _ and _
6 You can get very dirty and wet at _

5

ENGLISH YOU NEED

1 Write the questions in order.

1 some information / can you / please / give me / ? *Can you give me some information, please?*

2 to be / does / it / cost / how much / a member / ? ______

3 does / what / include / membership / ? ______

4 on anything / I / get / do / a discount / ? ______

5 you / be / do / 18 / to join / have to / ? ______

6 do / what / a member / I / do / have to / to become / ? ______

2 Match the questions with the answers.

a You can use all the facilities in the centre for free. ☐

b No, you can join when you're fifteen. ☐

c First, you have to complete this form with your details. ☐

d Yes, of course. How can I help you? *1*

e You pay 100 euros to join, and then 30 euros every month. ☐

f Yes, some of the things in our shop are cheaper for members. ☐

LISTENING

3 Read the job advertisement. Circle the true option and complete the sentence.

Summer jobs

Have fun working at our theme park this summer. Earn a salary. Free rides. One day off a week.

Call now: 071 465 5938

I'*d like* / *wouldn't like* a job at the theme park because ______

4 9 Listen to an interview for a job. Complete the director's form.

1 Name: *Helen* ______

2 Age: ______

3 Occupation: ______

4 Previous experience: Yes No

5 Free to work: July August September

6 Preferred work: ride operator storybook character

5 9 Listen again. Do you think Helen will accept the job? Why/Why not?

______

DICTATION

6 10 Listen. Write six sentences about Helen.

1 *She's* ______
2 ______
3 ______
4 ______
5 ______
6 ______

WRITING – A nomination

1 What does a teacher need to be like? Put them in order of importance.

_ strict
_ positive
_ organised
_ enthusiastic
_ fair

2 Read the email. Which qualities in exercise 1 does Fred's teacher have?

From: fred@teenmail.com
To:
Subject: My teacher

Hi guys!

I'm writing because nominations are open for the Local Hero Award. I'd like to nominate our French teacher because she's done a great job. At first I think she was a little frustrated because our French wasn't great. But we've all worked very hard because of her enthusiasm.

I know some of you think she's strict, but I think she's very reasonable. She never gets angry, and she's always fair. More than anything I think she deserves the award because her positive attitude has been an inspiration to us all.

If you agree, vote for Marie!

Fred

because v. *because of*

3 Write *of* if necessary.

1 I nominate my grandmother because x she's really generous.
2 I admire her because __ her energy.
3 We're very close because __ I see her most afternoons.
4 Another candidate is our doctor because __ his work for charity.
5 He spends the summer in Africa because __ people need his help.

4 Complete the sentences.

I'd like to nominate ______________________
because (of) ______________________
At first ______________________ but
____
I know some of you think ______________________
______________________ but ______________________
____
More than anything I think he / she deserves the award because (of) ______________________
____

CORRECTION

5 Correct the sentences.

1 Have ever you met my uncle? ✗
Have you ever met my uncle?
2 He's mechanic. ✗
____
3 He did a lot of jobs in his life. ✗
____
4 He's gone to a lot of countries too. ✗
____
5 My aunt's a membership of a travel club. ✗
____
____
6 They just have come back from Jordan. ✗
____
____

SELF CHECK 5

Jobs

1 Write the jobs. _ / 5

What job do I want to do? Mum's a (1) v _ _, but I don't really like animals. My dad's an (2) e _ _ _ _ _ _ _, but I haven't done well in my science exams this year. My aunt May's a (3) s _ _ _ _ _ w _ _ _ _ _, and she helps people with problems. I think that's interesting. But I really want to do something creative. I'd like to be an (4) a _ _ _ _ _ _ _ _, because I love drawing, or a (5) j _ _ _ _ _ _ _ _ _, because I love writing. What do you think?

Things people have done

2 Write the present perfect of the verbs. _ / 5

1 Madonna ____________ (make) a lot of good CDs.
2 What's her real name? I ____________ (forget) it.
3 We ________________ (not hear) her latest album.
4 It ____________ (sell) thousands of copies.
5 ________ you ________ (see) Madonna in concert?

Experiences and recent events

3 Complete the dialogue with the words below. _ / 5

never just been ever gone

A Where have you (1) ________ ? You weren't in the school canteen.
B I've (2) ________ had lunch with my mum in a Japanese restaurant. Have you (3) ________ eaten sushi?
A No. I've (4) ________ eaten Japanese food.
B It's really nice. Where's Jake?
A He's (5) ________ to the library. He's got some homework to finish.

Join a club

4 Circle the correct option. _ / 5

A Can I help you?
B Yes, we're interested in joining the club. What does family (1) *member* / *membership* include?
A You get a 50% discount on the (2) *enter* / *entry* price for a year.
B How old (3) *have you* / *do you have* to be (4) *for* / *to* join?
A If you come together, there are no age restrictions.
B And how much (5) *it costs* / *does it cost*?
A £350 for a family of four.

A local hero

5 Circle the correct option. _ / 5

My uncle Ray's a local hero. He works as a (1) … in a restaurant, but he's (2) … a lot of different jobs, so everyone knows him. He's very popular in the town because of (3) … . He's a really positive person too – (4) … heard him say a bad word about anyone. But he's a local hero (5) … he spends all his free time helping other people in the community.

1 a cooker b chef
2 a had b made
3 a he's funny b his sense of humour
4 a I never b I've never
5 a because b because of

➡ Answers page 118

6 Reference LIVING SPACE

GRAMMAR

First conditional

- A conditional sentence links two actions or events. If one action happens, the other action also happens.
  If Mark **finishes** work soon, he**'ll go** to the swimming pool.
- In conditional sentences, the possible action is the conditional clause, and the future result is the main clause. The word *if* introduces the conditional clause.

Conditional clause	Main clause
If we wait a bit longer,	we'll miss the traffic.

- We use the first conditional to refer to very probable consequences.
- We don't use *will/won't* in the conditional clause.
  If you **take** more exercise, you**'ll feel** fitter.
  NOT If you~~'ll~~ take more exercise …
- We use a comma to separate the two clauses when the *if* clause is at the beginning of the sentence. However, we can reverse the order of the clauses. When the *if* clause comes second, there is no comma.
  If you **take** more exercise, you**'ll feel** fitter.
  BUT You**'ll feel** fitter **if** you **take** more exercise.
- In negative first conditional sentences, the negative form can go in the conditional clause and/or the main clause.
  If she **isn't** careful, she**'ll have** an accident.
  She **won't have** an accident **if** she**'s** careful.
- We can also use the first conditional in questions.
  If we **wait** a bit longer, **will** we **miss** the traffic?
- We can also change the order of the clauses in first conditional questions.
  Will we **miss** the traffic **if** we **wait** a bit longer?

1 Link the two sentences or clauses in a conditional sentence.

1 Leave later. You'll miss the traffic.
If you leave later, you'll miss the traffic.

2 Eat something now. You won't be hungry later.
____

3 Learn a foreign language. You'll get a better job.
____

4 Give me your email address. We'll stay in contact.
____

5 Don't go to bed too late then you won't be tired tomorrow.
____

6 Listen or you won't understand the problem.
____

→ **Answers** page 116

Future time clauses

- When we talk about the future, we often use time clauses such as *when*, *until*, *before*, *after* and *as soon as*.
  We'll stay with you **until** you feel better.
- We use the future in the main clause and the present simple in the time clause.
  I'll go straight to bed **when** I **get** home.
  NOT … when I ~~will~~ get home.

- Except with *until*, we can reverse the order of the clauses. We use a comma after the time clause if it is at the beginning of the sentence.

  I'll call you **as soon as I'm** ready to leave.
  As soon as I'm ready to leave, **I'll call** you.

2 Put the words in order to make sentences in the future.

1 I / get home / call / you / when / I
I'll call you when I get home.

2 send / Patricia / she / an email / home / me / as soon as / arrive

3 I / until / home / my homework / finish / stay / I

4 to the campsite / put up / he / the tent / we / get / after

5 dad / ready / dinner / not be / before / arrive

6 finish / wait / until / she / the film

➟ **Answers** page 116

going to, will, might

going to

Affirmative	
Full form	Contracted form
I am going to eat. You are going to eat. He is going to eat. She is going to eat. It is going to eat.	I'm going to eat. You're going to eat. He's going to eat. She's going to eat. It's going to eat.
We are going to eat. You are going to eat. They are going to eat.	We're going to eat. You're going to eat. They're going to eat.

Negative	
Full form	Contracted form
I am not going to eat. You are not going to eat. He is not going to eat. She is not going to eat. It is not going to eat.	I'm not going to eat. You aren't going to eat. He isn't going to eat. She isn't going to eat. It isn't going to eat.
We are not going to eat. You are not going to eat. They are not going to eat.	We aren't going to eat. You aren't going to eat. They aren't going to eat.

Questions
Am I going to eat? Are you going to eat? Is he going to eat? Is she going to eat? Is it going to eat?
Are we going to eat? Are you going to eat? Are they going to eat?

Short answers	
Affirmative	Negative
Yes, I am. Yes, you are. Yes, he is. Yes, she is. Yes, it is.	No, I'm not. No, you aren't. No, he isn't. No, she isn't. No, it isn't.
Yes, we are. Yes, you are. Yes, they are.	No, we aren't. No, you aren't. No, they aren't.

- We use *be* + *going to* + infinitive to talk about:

  – an intention
  I'm going to repair the computer.

  – a predicted result based on evidence we can see now
  That wall**'s going to fall** down.

6 Reference

will

Affirmative	
Full form	Contracted form
I will win. You will win. He will win. She will win. It will win.	I'll win. You'll win. He'll win. She'll win. It'll win.
We will win. You will win. They will win.	We'll win. You'll win. They'll win.

Negative	
Full form	Contracted form
I will not win. You will not win. He will not win. She will not win. It will not win.	I won't win. You won't win. He won't win. She won't win. It won't win.
We will not win. You will not win. They will not win.	We won't win. You won't win. They won't win.

Questions
Will I win? Will you win? Will he win? Will she win? Will it win?
Will we win? Will you win? Will they win?

Short answers	
Affirmative	Negative
Yes, I will. Yes, you will. Yes, he will. Yes, she will. Yes, it will.	No, I won't. No, you won't. No, he won't. No, she won't. No, it won't.
Yes, we will. Yes, you will. Yes, they will.	No, we won't. No, you won't. No, they won't.

- We use *will/won't* + infinitive to talk about:

  – future facts in general
  The financial crisis **will cause** problems for many people.

  – predictions
  I think they**'ll build** a new bridge in 2015.

might

- *Might* expresses a more remote possibility that something could happen than *will probably*.
  You**'ll probably** be tired after the long journey. (a logical conclusion)
  You **might** be tired after the journey. (not very certain at all)
- *Might* is a modal verb, and therefore the form is the same for all persons.
  You **might meet** Brad next week.
  She **might finish** her homework soon.
- *Might* is always followed by the infinitive without *to*.
  I **might try** something different on the menu.
  NOT I might ~~to~~ try …
- The interrogative form *Might I, you*, etc. is not normally used.

3 Complete the dialogue with *will, probably won't, might* or *going to.*

A I (**1**) _'m going to_ watch a film later tonight on TV, but I (**2**) ________________ watch it all, especially if I start feeling tired.

B You could watch it on the internet tomorrow.

A I (**3**) ________ do that. Do you think that in fifty years' time (**4**) they ________ send TV programmes straight to our brains?

B Maybe, but when (**5**) ________ we find the time to work?

A People (**6**) ________________ work by then!

➟ **Answers** page 116

6 Reference

VOCABULARY

Student's Multi-ROM Speaking dictionary

Bedroom objects

armchair	/ˈɑːmtʃeə/	______
bedside table	/ˈbedsaɪd ˈteɪbl/	______
blind	/blaɪnd/	______
bookcase	/ˈbʊkkeɪs/	______
chest of drawers	/tʃest əv drɔːz/	______
drawer	/drɔː/	______
fan	/fæn/	______
noticeboard	/ˈnəʊtɪsbɔːd/	______
stool	/stuːl/	______
wastepaper bin	/weɪstˈpeɪpə bɪn/	______

The environment

collect rainwater	/kəˈlekt ˈreɪnwɔːtə/	______
generate electricity	/ˈdʒenəreɪt ɪlekˈtrɪsəti/	______
install solar panels	/ɪnˈstɔːl ˈsəʊlə ˈpænls/	______
insulate windows	/ˈɪnsjuleɪt ˈwɪndəʊz/	______
recycle glass and paper	/riːˈsaɪkl glaːz ənd ˈpeɪpə/	______
re-use containers	/riːˈjuːz kənˈteɪnəz/	______
save energy	/seɪv ˈenədʒi/	______
use wind power	/juːˈz wɪnd ˈpaʊə/	______

English you need

- Get around in a new place.

Go along this street until you get to the traffic lights.

______

Turn left.

______

Take the second turning on the right.

______

Keep going and you'll see it in front of you.

______

It's on the corner.

______

It's on the left.

______

Learning tip

- Listing different categories can help you remember words.

1 Match each word with the category.

armchair shirt hoodie library card ~~sofa~~ membership card litter sweatshirt junk

1 chairs: *sofa* ______
2 cards: ______
3 rubbish: ______
4 tops: ______

2 Write two types of each thing.

1 books: ______
2 shoes: ______
3 energy: ______
4 art: ______

➟ **Answers** page 116

6 LIVING SPACE

VOCABULARY – Bedroom objects

1 Look at the pictures. Find the bedroom objects in the wordsearch.

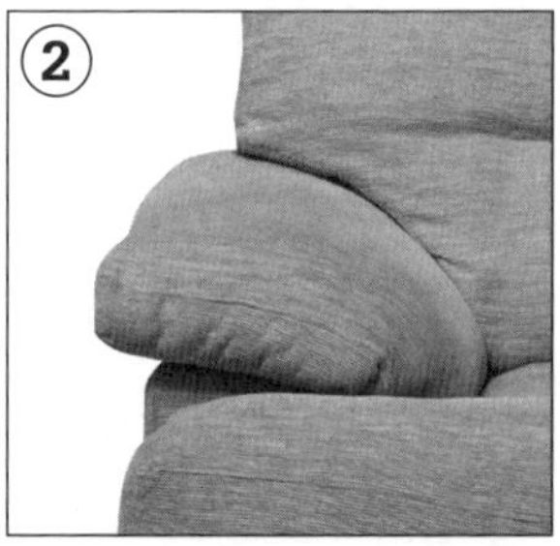

A	G	C	O	A	R	M	C	H	A	I	R	F
W	V	H	F	L	D	R	A	W	E	R	I	W
I	B	E	D	W	E	C	H	A	I	R	N	A
N	E	S	T	O	O	L	X	S	D	O	O	R
D	M	T	M	P	L	A	N	T	R	B	T	D
O	B	O	O	K	C	A	S	E	G	S	I	R
W	U	F	T	Q	L	A	M	P	R	K	C	O
B	E	D	S	I	D	E	T	A	B	L	E	B
L	V	R	U	L	B	H	Q	P	X	B	B	E
I	N	A	D	A	Y	S	H	E	L	F	O	S
N	A	W	C	W	M	I	R	R	O	R	A	H
D	D	E	S	K	C	U	P	B	O	A	R	D
C	A	R	P	E	T	K	J	I	N	Y	D	C
D	I	S	T	P	Z	F	A	N	J	Z	O	P

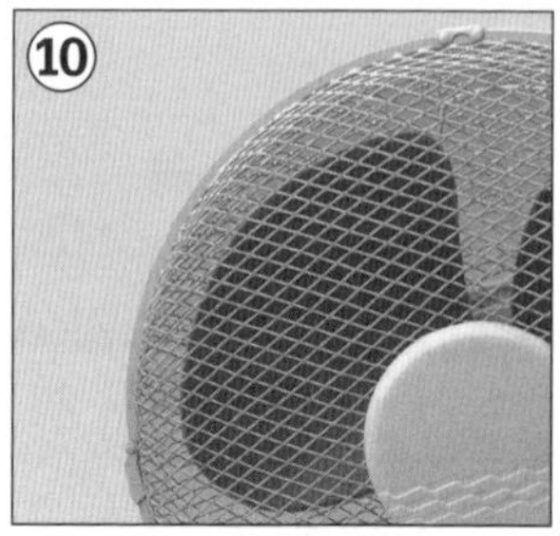

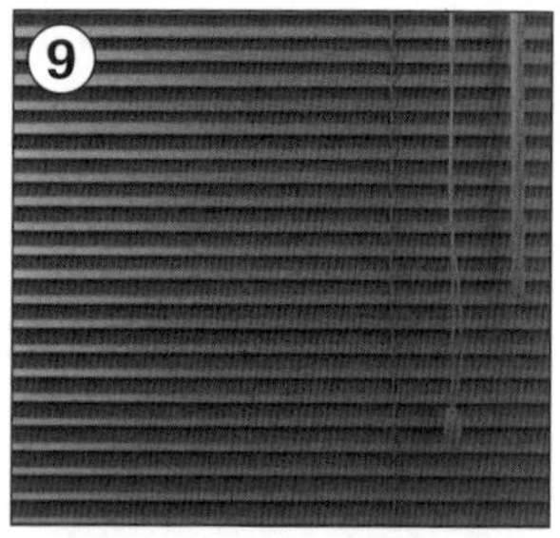

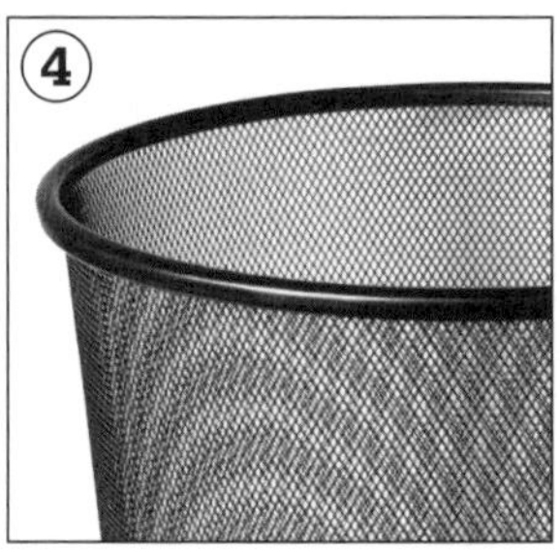

2 Can you find twelve more bedroom objects?

window, ______________________________

GRAMMAR

First conditional

1 Circle the correct option.

Six ways to keep 'chi', or life energy, moving around your home

1 If there *'s* / *will be* plenty of light in the entrance, chi *comes* / *will come* into the house.

2 If you *put* / *'ll put* a mirror opposite the door, it *reflects* / *will reflect* chi out of your house.

3 You *'re* / *'ll be* lucky if you *have* / *'ll have* an aquarium in the living room.

4 Chi *doesn't move* / *won't move* easily if you *don't put* / *won't put* lights in dark corners.

5 If you *don't throw* / *won't throw* dry flowers away, they *accumulate* / *'ll accumulate* negative energy.

6 Electromagnetic waves *destroy* / *will destroy* chi if your sound system *'s* / *will be* in a prominent position.

2 Write questions in the first conditional. Then answer them.

1 you / read / in bed / you / not feel / tired tonight ?
Will you read in bed if you don't feel tired tonight?
Yes, I will.

2 what / you / do / the weather / be / good next weekend ?
____
____
____

3 your family / have / a summer holiday / where / you / go?
____
____
____

4 your friends / not meet / on Saturday evening, / you / stay / at home ?
____
____
____

5 what / you / study / you / go / to university ?
____
____
____

6 your next class / not finish / on time / what / you / say ?
____
____
____

Future time clauses

3 Complete the sentences for you. Use *will*, *won't* or the present simple.

1 *I'll play computer games* when I finish my homework.

2 I ________________________ after I have dinner.

3 As soon as I get up tomorrow, ________________________

4 I'll probably have a big party when ________________________

5 I won't get married until ________________________

6 ________________________ before I'm thirty years old.

VOCABULARY – The environment

1 Write eight ways to protect the environment. Use words and phrases in the boxes.

insulate recycle use generate
re-use collect install ~~save~~

solar panels ~~energy~~ wind power
glass and paper windows electricity
containers rainwater

Ways to protect the environment:

1 *Save energy.*
2 ______
3 ______
4 ______
5 ______
6 ______
7 ______
8 ______

2 What do you and your family do to protect the environment? Use words in exercise 1 and other ideas.

1 *We don't use a lot of plastic bags.*
2 ______
3 ______
4 ______

GRAMMAR – *going to, will, might*

3 Write the family's plans and intentions with *going to*.

Don't waste paper!

Don't use plastic bags!

Switch off the lights!

Don't drop litter!

Spend less time in the shower!

Recycle batteries!

1 I *'m not going to waste paper.*
2 My mum ______
3 My sister ______
4 We ______
5 I ______
6 They ______

4 Choose the best option.

In the future we (1) *'re going to* / *will* do more things to protect the environment. I (2) *'m going to* / *will* turn off the water when I clean my teeth. This (3) *is going to* / *will* save water. My mum (4) *isn't going to* / *won't* throw away paper and glass. And we (5) *aren't going to* / *won't* have enough oil in the world in fifty years' time so my dad (6) *'s going to* / *will* cycle to work every day.

5 Write the words in order about the future home.

1 might / robots / our meals / prepare
Robots might prepare our meals.

2 the rubbish / probably / will / our waste bins / divide

____

____

3 in an oxygen tent / probably / we / sleep / won't

____

____

4 will / switch on and off automatically / lights in the house / probably

____

____

____

5 very thin / might / the TV screen / be

____

____

6 a computer / probably / the bathroom mirror / won't / be

____

____

6 Write about Jon's future. Use *will probably*, *might* or *probably won't*.

I think so
have children
be a mechanic

It's possible
live in the country
visit the USA

I don't think so
be rich and famous
travel in space

1 *He'll probably have children.*
2 ____________________
3 ____________________
4 ____________________
5 ____________________
____
6 ____________________
____

7 Match the parts of the sentences about next weekend.

1	I'm going	**a**	won't get up early.
2	I'll	**b**	going to watch TV.
3	I might	**c**	probably meet friends.
4	I probably	**d**	to go swimming.
5	I'm not	**e**	go to the cinema.

8 Write five different sentences about your plans for the summer holidays.

1 ____________________
2 ____________________
3 ____________________
4 ____________________
5 ____________________

READING

1 Can you choose the correct options about the people in the photo?

1 There are about a *hundred / thousand* tribes like this in the world.
2 Most of them live in *Europe / South America*.
3 They *want / don't want* contact with the outside world.

2 Read the article and check your answers.

Hiding from the outside world

We know almost all of the different people and cultures around the world. However, according to human rights organisation Survival International, there are about 100 *lost* tribes. More than half of them live in Brazil or Peru.

In 2008, the Brazilian government took photographs of one of these tribes from an aeroplane. It lives in the Amazon rainforest. The government published the photos to show that the tribe's land needs protection.

The photographs give us an idea of how these tribes live. There are communal buildings, probably with hammocks for sleeping in. And although the tribe kills wild animals, it grows some food too. The photos also suggest that the tribe is hiding.

Tribes hide for a number of reasons. Some think that if they hide, they won't lose their land. A lot hide because they have no defence against illnesses like colds and flu. If they have contact with other people, they might die.

How long will indigenous tribes like this survive? If we leave them alone, they might have a chance.

3 Read again and answer the questions.

1 How many 'lost' tribes are there in Brazil and Peru?
More than 50.
2 Where does the tribe in the photograph live?
____
3 Why did the Brazilian government publish photographs of the tribe?
____
4 How does the tribe get its food?
____
5 What might happen if these tribes don't hide?
____
6 What will happen if we leave them alone?
____

ENGLISH YOU NEED

1 Complete the dialogue.

A Excuse me. (1) W _e're_ l _ _ _ _ _ _ f _ _ the Forum. (2) I _ t _ _ _ n _ _ _ h _ _ _?

B No, it's in the city centre.

A (3) W _ _ _ _ b _ _ g _ _ _ t _ the centre?

B The number 63.

A (4) I _ t _ _ _ _ a b _ _ s _ _ _ near here?

B Yes. It's not far.

2 Put the words in order to make directions. Then circle the bus stop on the map.

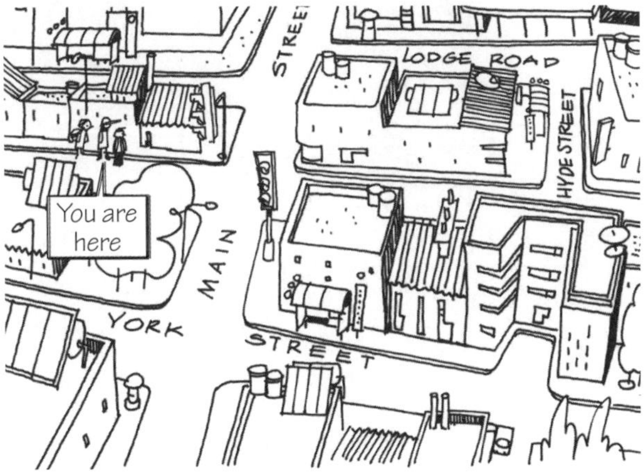

1 until / Go / to / the traffic lights / along / you / this street / get
Go along ______

______

2 take / on the right / Turn / the first turning / and then / left

______

______

3 on / it / you'll / going / the right / Keep / and / see

______

______

4 Lodge Road / of / It's / the corner / on / Hyde Street / and

______

______

LISTENING

3 11 Can you choose the correct options about the Yanomami tribe. Listen and check.

1 They live in *Alaska* / *Brazil and Venezuela*.
2 They live in *houses* / *tents*.
3 Their population is *3,200* / *32,000*.
4 People are *buying* / *destroying* their land.

4 11 Listen again and complete the notes.

The Yanomami live in (1) _rainforests_ and _mountains_. Their (2) ______ are called 'yanos'. Up to (3) ______ people can live in one. They grow food but also eat (4) ______ and ______. They make (5) ______ together – they believe in equality.

If we don't help them, they (6) ______ ______.

DICTATION

5 12 Listen. Write six sentences about a future home.

1 _Don't_ ______
______
2 ______
______
3 ______
______
4 ______
5 ______
6 ______
______

WRITING – My predictions

1 What's your opinion about travel in the future? Circle one option.

1 People *will* / *might* travel to space on holiday.
2 People will travel abroad *more* / *less*.
3 Air travel will be *cheaper* / *more expensive*.

Presenting ideas

2 Read the composition. Write the words and phrases. Are the opinions the same?

On the one hand   In conclusion
~~However~~   On the other hand

A lot of people go on holiday abroad now because air travel is cheap. (1) *However*, the price of oil is increasing and this will probably change the way we travel in the future.
(2) ______________, I'm sure that people will continue to visit other parts of the world. Some people might also travel to space on holiday.
(3) ______________, I think that people will travel less often. If we don't find other forms of energy, air travel will be too expensive for most people.
(4) ______________, people will probably continue to travel, but less than now.

3 Write about local transport in the future. Use these and your own ideas.

cars – price of oil
public transport – alternative means of transport

People use cars all the time now. In the future ...

____

____

____

____

____

____

TRANSLATION

4 Translate the sentences.

1 You won't sleep if you've got a mirror in your room. ______________
2 I'll call you as soon as I get home. ______________
3 We're going to install solar panels. ______________
4 People might live in an 'i-Home' one day. ______________
5 Excuse me. Is there a bus stop near here? ______________
6 Keep going and then turn right. ______________

SELF CHECK 6

Bedroom objects

1 Write the words in the description. _ / 5

There's a wardrobe in my bedroom. I keep some clothes in the wardrobe, and the rest in a (1) ________________ . I've got a (2) ________________ for my alarm clock and lamp. There isn't an (3) ____________ in my room because I usually lie on my bed to relax. But there's a desk and a (4) ____________ to sit on. At the window, I haven't got curtains, I've got a (5) ____________

Feng shui

2 Write the verbs in the first conditional. _ / 5

1 You ____________ (see) things more easily if you ____________ (clean) your mirror.
2 You ____________ (not sleep) well if your bed ____________ (have got) junk under it.
3 If the walls ____________ (be) a light colour, you ____________ (feel) more relaxed.
4 If you ____________ (not open) your window, fresh 'chi' ________________ (not come) in.
5 If you ____________ (have got) a lot of books on your bedside table, they ____________ (disturb) your sleep.

The future home

3 Choose the best option. _ / 5

Today, I (1) … talk to you about the home of the future. I'm sure it (2) … be very different from now. For example, it (3) … be more environmentally-friendly. Some people think we (4) … build houses from recycled material. I don't know about that, but I think the future home (5) … have light switches because the lights will turn on and off automatically.

	a	b
1	a will	b 'm going to
2	a will	b might
3	a will probably	b probably will
4	a might	b going to
5	a won't probably	b probably won't

Get around in a new place

4 Write one word in each space. _ / 5

keep turn turning on along

A Excuse me. Is there an Internet café near here?
B Yes, there is. Go (1) ________ this street and take the first (2) ________ on the left. (3) ________ going until you get to some traffic lights. Then (4) ________ right. You'll see the Internet café (5) ________ the right.
A Thank you.

An opinion about the future

5 Complete the words. _ / 5

A lot of schools have computers.
(1) H _ _ _ _ _ _, I think technology will be more important in the future.
(2) O _ _ _ _ _ _ _ _ _ _ _, I think students will continue to go to school, but they (3) m _ _ _ _ not go every day.
(4) O _ _ _ _ _ _ _ _ _ _ _ _ _ _ _, the lessons probably won't be the same. Students will probably study all their lessons on a computer.
(5) I _ _ _ _ _ _ _ _ _ _ _ _, I think schools will continue to exist but how students study will be different.

➡ **Answers** page 118

COLLECTIONS

GRAMMAR

Present perfect with *for/since*

- We often use the present perfect with the time expressions *for* and *since* to say how long a situation has continued for.
  Neil **hasn't returned** to Ireland **for** two years.
  Janet **has taught** English **since** 2004.
- *For* is used with a period of time, e.g. minutes, hours, days, weeks, months, years.
  I've lived here **for ten years**.
  We **haven't seen** each other **for a long time**.
  NOT ... ~~since~~ a long time
- *Since* is used with a specific point in the past, e.g. a time, date or year.
  I've lived here **since 1999**.
  We **haven't seen** each other **since January**.
- After *since* we can also use a clause.
  She**'s worked** in this area **since she was twenty**.

1 Complete the sentences. Use the present perfect and *for* or *since*.

1 Marcia *has lived* (live) in Newcastle *for* eight years.
2 I ______ (work) in Rome ______ last summer.
3 Paul ______ (not see) Alison ______ long time.
4 ______ you ______ (talk) to John ______ Friday?
5 They ______ (not have) fish and chips ______ they were in London.
6 We ______ (be) in the park ______ two hours.

➟ **Answers** page 116

How long?

- We use *How long?* with the present perfect to ask about the period of time an action or situation has continued up to the present.
  How long have you **had** that watch?
- We generally use *for* or *since* to answer questions with *How long?*
  How long has Margaret **worked** as a secretary?
  She**'s worked** as a secretary **for** two years.

  How long have you **known** Peter?
  I've known him **since** last summer.

2 Look at the table and complete the questions and answers.

Mark Thomas is 32. It is Friday 12th June 2009.

Activity	Age
starts playing football	7
starts liking art	13
meets Cheryl	23
becomes a doctor	25
gets married	26
buys a new watch	27

1 How long / Mark / play / football ?
How long has Mark played football?
Since he was 7.

2 How long / Mark / like / art ?
____
____

3 How long / he / know / Cheryl ?
____
____

4 How long / he / be / a doctor ?
____
____

5 How long / he / be / married ?
____
____

6 How long / he / have / that watch ?
____
____

➞ **Answers** page 116

Present perfect v. past simple

Present perfect

To talk about actions that happened in the past but not when they happened.
Carrie **has stayed** at that hotel twice.

For situations that began in the past and continue up to the present moment.
Freda **has worked** here **for several years**.

With time expressions such as:
- *since* + day, date, month, year or clause
- *for* + period of time

With an incomplete time expression such as *today*, *this week*, *this month*, *recently*, etc.
John**'s had** two cups of tea **today**.

Past simple

To talk about actions that happened at a specific point in the past.
Lee **went** to Portugal **last year**.

For situations that happened in a period of time that has ended.
I **lived** in Germany **from 2002 to 2006**.

With time expressions such as:
- *in* + year
- *on* + day or date
- *at* + time
- after *when*
- *last* + week, month, year
- *for* + period of time

3 Choose the correct past simple or present perfect verb.

~~played~~ 've worn haven't seen 's played wore didn't see

1 Mr Franks died at the age of 91. He *played* football all his life.
2 He ______ cards for as long as he can remember.
3 We ______ you at the cinema last week.
4 I ______ a film at the cinema for ages.
5 Those women ______ the same dress to a party recently.
6 Do you need some new clothes? You ______ the same thing for the past three days.

➡ **Answers** page 116

VOCABULARY

Student's Multi-ROM Speaking dictionary

Sports equipment

basket	/'bɑːskɪt/	______
bat	/bæt/	______
gloves	/glʌvs/	______
goal	/gəʊl/	______
goggles	/'gɒglz/	______
helmet	/'helmɪt/	______
ice-skates	/'aɪskeɪts/	______
knee pads	/niː pæds/	______
net	/net/	______
racket	/'rækɪt/	______
skis	/skiːz/	______
stick	/stɪk/	______

Life box

autograph book	/'ɔːtəgrɑːf bʊk/	______
badges	/'bædʒɪz/	______
bracelet	/'breɪslət/	______
concert ticket	/'kɒnsət 'tɪkɪt/	______
key ring	/kiː rɪŋ/	______
mug	/mʌg/	______
scarf	/skɑːf/	______
school certificate	/skuːl sə'tɪfɪkət/	______
teddy bear	/'tedi beə/	______
wallet	/'wɒlɪt/	______

English you need

- Complain

I'm calling about a tracksuit I ordered.

___

It isn't the one I ordered.

___

I'm sorry about that.

___

We'll send you a new one today.

___

I'd like to change it.

___

What's wrong with it exactly?

___

It doesn't work.

___

Have you got the receipt?

___

Learning tip

- We don't pronounce some letters in English words. It's a good idea to notice these silent letters.

1 Write the silent letter (or letters) in these words.

1 knee pad _k_
2 answer ___
3 write ___
4 island ___
5 honest ___
6 walked ___

2 Underline the silent letter in these words.

1 climb
2 listen
3 ironing
4 knock
5 building
6 vegetable

→ **Answers** page 116

7 COLLECTIONS

VOCABULARY Sports equipment

1 Complete the words.

1 s*kis*
2 g _ _ _ _ _ _
3 b _ _ _ _ _
4 h _ _ _ _ _
5 g _ _ _ _ _
6 k _ _ _ p _ _ _
7 i _ _ s _ _ _ _ _
8 s _ _ _ _
9 g _ _ _
10 r _ _ _ _ _
11 n _ _
12 b _ _

2 Read the clues and circle the odd word.

1	skis	ice-skates	(racket)	trainers	You wear the other things on your feet.
2	racket	bat	stick	goal	You hit the ball with the other things.
3	goggles	net	helmet	hat	You wear the other things on your head.
4	knee pads	court	pitch	swimming pool	You do sport on or in the other things.
5	goal	gloves	basket	net	You don't wear the other things.
6	football	skiing	ice-hockey	water polo	The other things are team sports.

3 Write about sports you play and the equipment you use.

I sometimes go swimming at school, and I use goggles.

____

____

____

7

GRAMMAR Present perfect with *for/since*

1 Write the verbs in the present perfect. Then match parts of the sentences.

1 e 3 _ 5 _
2 _ 4 _ 6 _

1 In the USA, people have played (play)
2 Baseball ______________ (have) its modern rules since
3 According to some experts, Nordic people ______________ (use) skis for
4 Downhill skiing ______________ (be)
5 The Japanese ______________ (practise)
6 Since the first game in 1967, the Super Bowl ______________ (become)

a 7,000 years.
b the most popular TV event in the USA.
c a sport at the Winter Olympics since 1936.
d 1845.
e water polo for over a century.
f martial arts for centuries.

2 Write the words in the table.

~~Saturday~~ six days a long time I was ten
1962 last week April a month eight years

for	since
	Saturday

3 Circle the correct option.

My hobby's water polo. I've loved swimming (1) *for* / *since* I was a child, but I haven't been interested in water polo (2) *for* / *since* a long time. It all started when I met Dimitri. He's played (3) *for* / *since* he was five. He's from Russia, but he's lived in the UK (4) *for* / *since* 2007. He joined a water-polo team here, and encouraged me to play. My city's only had a water-polo club (5) *for* / *since* a short time, and I've been a member (6) *for* / *since* last July.

4 Write sentences with the present perfect and *for* or *since*. Who are the people?

1 He / be / a superstar / a long time
He's been a superstar for a long time.
2 He / play / football / he was a boy
____
3 He / not play / in England / 2003
____
4 She / not recorded any new / albums / years
____
5 She / become / a style icon / she stopped making music
____
6 They / be / married / more than ten years
____

Who are they? ______________

VOCABULARY – Life box

1 Do the puzzle.

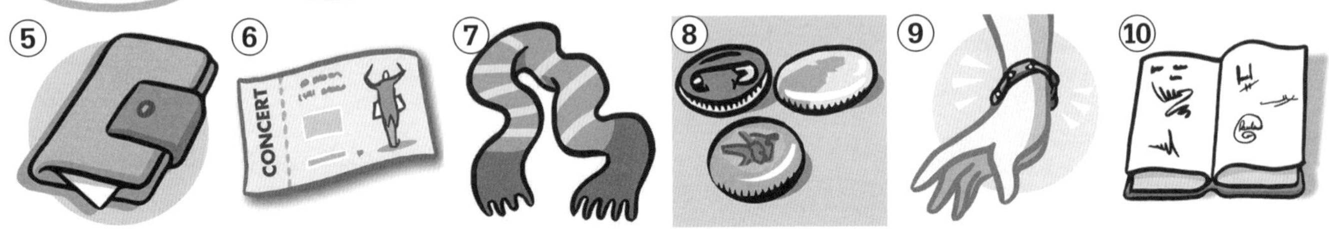

2 Write true sentences about the objects.

1 I've got ____________________. It's ____________________

I like it because ____________________

2 I've also got ____________________

3 One of my favourite objects is ____________________

4 I haven't got ____________________

GRAMMAR – *How long?*

3 Write questions with *How long*? Then answer the questions with *for* or *since*.

1 live in the same town or city
2 have your mobile phone
3 receive pocket money
4 be a teenager
5 like your favourite TV programme
6 know your English teacher

1 *How long have you lived in the same town or city* ? *Since I was born.*
2 ____________________ ? __________
3 ____________________ ? __________
4 ____________________ ? __________
5 ____________________ ? __________
6 ____________________ ? __________

4 Read about Erica's life box. Then write the questions.

These are photos of my parents in Mexico. They moved to the USA sixteen years ago. My parents gave this teddy bear to me when I was a baby. And this bracelet was a present from my friend Lily. I'm fifteen now, and I've known her since I was five. My cousins sent me this autograph book from Spain. They've been there since 2006 so I don't see them very often. I've done tai chi for three years so I've got some certificates from that. And this is a ticket from a Rihanna concert. I'm a big fan since I saw her in concert.

1 *How long have her parents lived in the USA?*
For sixteen years.

2 ____________________
Since she was a baby.

3 ____________________
For ten years.

4 ____________________
____
Since 2006.

5 ____________________
For three years.

6 ____________________
Since Erica saw her in concert.

5 Write the correct word in the sentences.

last since for in when ~~since~~

1 We've lived at our present address *since* 2008.
2 My mum's worn glasses ________ a year.
3 I got this scarf for Christmas ________ year.
4 My dad gave me this bracelet ________ 2006.
5 I've known my best friend ________ we were at primary school.
6 My gran took this photo of me ________ I was ten.

Present perfect v. past simple

6 Write the verbs in the past simple or present perfect.

Rihanna (1) *was born* (be born) in Barbados but she (2) ____________ (live) in the USA for some years. She (3) ____________ (get) her big break in 2003 when she (4) ____________ (meet) music producer Evan Rogers. Since her debut in 2005, she (5) ____________ (make) a number of albums. And she (6) ____________ (sing) in concerts all over the world.

7 Complete the second sentence so it means the same as the first.

1 My brother started collecting coins when he was ten.
My brother *'s collected* coins since he was ten.

2 My mum gave my life box to me when I was five.
I've had my life box ________________ five.

3 My cousin went to live in the USA last year.
My cousin ________________ in the USA for a year.

4 We met our neighbours five years ago.
We've known our neighbours ____________
____

5 I started playing the guitar in 2006.
I ________________________ 2006.

READING

1 Can you match the things with the people? Read and check.

1 ___Cher___'s wig.
2 ________________'s jacket.
3 A concert ticket to see ________________
4 ________________'s skirt.

David Beckham

Avril Lavigne

Alicia Keys

Cher

Celebrity auctions

More and more people today sell objects at Internet auction sites. Believe it or not, celebrities auction their old things too. Recently, Cher decided to clean her house. She sold dresses, jewellery, a wig and even a bed! She made 3.5 million dollars, and donated some of the money to charity.

Internet auctions are now a popular way for celebrities to make money for charities. They donate autographs or clothes and people bid to buy them. The person with the highest bid receives the object, and the money goes to help people in need. In recent years, Avril Lavigne's skirt and David Beckham's leather jacket have both appeared at Internet auctions.

Celebrities also donate their time or skills. Past auctions have included a tennis lesson with Serena Williams, lunch with Bill Clinton and the chance to meet Alicia Keys after her concert. More unusual donations have been the promise to write a short story about a pet, and a personalised tattoo design.

The good thing about celebrity auctions is that everyone benefits. People have something from their favourite star and charities raise money to help people all over the world.

2 Read again and answer the questions.

1 What did Cher sell in her auction?
She sold dresses, jewellery, a wig and a bed.

2 Did she donate all the money to charity?
____

3 What objects do celebrities often donate?
____

4 Who receives the object?
____

5 What other things do celebrities donate?
____

6 What do charities do with the money?
____

ENGLISH YOU NEED

1 Match the parts of the sentences.

1 It doesn't — a change it.
2 I'm sorry — b work.
3 I'm calling about — c a new one.
4 I'd like to — d I ordered.
5 We'll send you — e about that.
6 It isn't the one — f a camera I ordered.

2 Complete the conversation with an online shop with sentences from exercise 1.

A Customer services. Can I help you?
B (1) *I'm calling about a camera I ordered.*
A What's wrong with it?
B Two things. First of all, (2) ______________________

____
I ordered a red one, and you sent me a blue one.
A (3) ______________________
What's the other problem?
B (4) ______________________
When you press the button, nothing happens. So (5) ______________________
A (6) ______________________
Can you give me your details?
B Yes. My name's Sandra …

LISTENING

3 13 Sandra's returning something to a shop. Listen and answer the questions.

1 What's she returning?
____
2 What was wrong with it?
____
3 What does the shop do?
____

4 13 True or false? Correct the false sentences.

1 The jumper isn't Sandra's normal size.
False. It's her normal size, but it's big.
2 She wants to change the jumper.
____
3 She's had the jumper for a week.
____
4 She bought the jumper.
____
5 The shop doesn't sell the jumper now.
____
6 Sandra's got the receipt.
____

DICTATION

5 14 Listen. Write six sentences about Sandra and her things.

1 *My family*
2 ______________________
____
3 ______________________
4 ______________________
____
5 ______________________
____
6 ______________________

WRITING – My collection

1 Which things do you collect? Tick (✓) the things.

1 posters _
2 postcards _
3 comics _
4 CDs / music _
5 photos _
6 computer games _

2 Read about the boy's collection. Answer the questions.

1 What does he collect? ____________

2 What three types has he got? ____________

I collect postcards. I've collected them since I was really young. I started because my grandparents always sent cards from their holidays. Now I've got hundreds.

I've got a lot of postcards from different countries, like Holland, Australia and Japan. My favourite is from Thailand because it's very beautiful.

I also collect old postcards. I like them because they show places in the past such as New York or London in the 1900s.

I've got a special collection of funny postcards too, for example, postcards of animals. They always make me laugh!

Examples

3 Circle the ways of giving examples in the text in exercise 2. Then complete the sentences.

1 I like adventure sports, l*ike* *rafting and rock climbing.*

2 I listen to a lot of music s________ a________

3 I read magazines, l________ ________

4 I love buying clothes, f________ ________

4 Write about your collection.

I collect ____________

CORRECTION

5 Correct the sentences.

1 People play tennis for 500 years. ✗

2 I've had a skateboard since five years. ✗

3 We've lived in this city from 2002. ✗

4 How much time have you been a student? ✗

5 You can't change it without the ticket. ✗

6 I collect comics as manga. ✗

Sports equipment

1 Complete with sports equipment. _ / 5

Ice hockey's a great sport. You hit a ball called a 'puck' with a (1) ________ and it goes very fast. It's very physical, so you need to wear protection. I always wear a (2) ________ on my head, knee (3) ________, and (4) ________ to protect my hands. And you need to wear ice (5) ________ on your feet, of course!

The history of sports

2 Choose the correct option. _ / 5

Water polo developed in England and Scotland. The basic rules of the game (1) … a lot (2) … 1888, when the London Water Polo League approved them. Since the 19th century, water polo (3) … popular in many European countries and in the USA. It has been an Olympic sport for (4) …, but women's teams have only played at the Olympics (5) … the Sydney games in 2000.

1 **a** don't change **b** haven't changed
2 **a** for **b** since
3 **a** has become **b** became
4 **a** 1900 **b** about a hundred years
5 **a** for **b** since

Talk about how long

3 Complete the dialogue. _ / 5

A (1) ______________________ (you / know) Julie?

B For three years. I (2) ________ (meet) her at school.

A (3) ______________________ (she / be) in Manchester? She hasn't got a Manchester accent.

B She (4) ______________________ (not live) here all her life. Her family (5) ________ (come) to live here six years ago.

Complain

4 Circle the correct option. _ / 5

A Can I help you?

B Yes, it's this mobile. I'd like (1) *change / to change* it.

A What's (2) *happen / wrong* with it?

B It doesn't (3) *function / work*.

A I'm sorry (4) *about / for* that. Have you got the (5) *receipt / ticket*?

B Yes. Here you are.

A collection

5 Write the words. _ / 5

I collect things from different places, (1) l _ _ _ postcards and stamps. I also collect Spider-Man things (2) s _ _ _ a _ comics and posters. I'm a fan of Chelsea football club, so I collect Chelsea things, (3) f _ _ e _ _ _ _ _ _ shirts. I've also got players' names in my (4) a _ _ _ _ _ _ _ _ b _ _ _. But I've only got one Chelsea (5) s _ _ _ _. My grandad gave it to me and I wear it round my neck to every match.

➡ **Answers** page 118

8 Reference

ACTION!

GRAMMAR

Present and past passive: affirmative

Present passive

Subject	*be*	past participle	agent
The soundtrack	is	played	by a pianist.
The students	are	helped	by a teacher.

Past passive

Subject	*be*	past participle	agent
The window	was	opened	by Matthew.
Those films	were	directed	by Coppola.

- We form the passive with the verb *be* and the past participle of the main verb.
  We **are paid** every month.
  The mobile phone **wasn't invented** until the twentieth century.
- The passive is very common in English. We use it particularly when we want to give more importance to the action than to the person or thing performing the action (the agent).
- We usually omit *by* + the agent when it is not important.
  The bridge was completed in 1850.
  The bridge was completed (by them) in 1850.

1 Four of the following sentences are wrong. Correct them if necessary.

1 The play is base on a famous novel.
The play is based on a famous novel.

2 The man was seen in various parts of town.

____

3 This watch is repaired last Christmas.

____

4 Some actors are only chosen for their good looks.

____

5 The sandwich was eaten for Pam.

____

6 This car were built by robots.

____

➟ **Answers** page 116

Present and past passive: negative

Present passive

Subject	*be not*	past participle	agent
The song	isn't	sung	by Beyoncé.
The expenses	aren't	paid	by a company.

Past passive

Subject	*be not*	past participle	agent
The tower	wasn't	built	by Calatrava.
They	weren't	invited	by your friend.

2 Make the sentences in Exercise 1 negative.

1 *The play isn't based on a famous novel.*
2 ______
3 ______
4 ______
5 ______
6 ______

➟ **Answers** page 116

Active v. passive

- In a passive sentence, the direct object of the active sentence becomes the subject of the passive sentence. The subject of the active sentence can appear as the agent of the action, introduced by the preposition *by*.
  Active: **Hitchcock** directed **the film**.
  Passive: **The film** was directed **by Hitchcock**.
- In active sentences, if the agent is not known, or is not important, we can say *They* ... or *People* ... + active verb.
  Active: **They completed** the bridge in two years.
  Passive: The bridge **was completed** in two years.
  Active: **People used** tapes to listen to music some years ago.
  Passive: Tapes **were used** to listen to music some years ago.

3 Make the active sentences passive.

1 People stole many Egyptian artefacts.
Many Egyptian artefacts were stolen.
2 This actor won several awards last year.
______
3 William didn't tell the truth.
______
4 Holbein painted many royal portraits.
______
5 A foreign collector bought the watch.
______
6 John McAdam invented tarmac.
______

➟ **Answers** page 116

8 Reference

VOCABULARY

Student's Multi-ROM Speaking dictionary

Film genres

adventure	/əd'ventʃə/	________
animation	/ænɪ'meɪʃən/	________
comedy	/'kɒmədi/	________
crime	/kraɪm/	________
drama	/'drɑːmə/	________
fantasy	/'fæntəsi/	________
horror	/'hɒrə/	________
musical	/'mjuːzɪkəl/	________
romance	/'rəʊmæns/	________
science fiction	/saɪəns'fɪkʃən/	________
thriller	/'θrɪlə/	________
war	/w ɔː/	________

Behind the camera

cast	/kɑːst/	________
costumes	/'kɒstjuːmz/	________
director	/də'rektə/	________
make-up	/'meɪkʌp/	________
photography	/fə'tɒgrəfi/	________
script	/skrɪpt/	________
soundtrack	/'saʊndtræk/	________
special effects	/'speʃl ɪ'fekts/	________

English you need

- Make recommendations

I don't think you should get her that.

____

So what do you recommend?

____

Oh, you must see it.

____

I'm not convinced.

____

Because I really recommend *The Others*.

____

Maybe I shouldn't get her a film. Maybe I should get her a CD.

____

____

That's not a bad idea.

____

Learning tip

- It's important to notice how two words can combine to make a new word.

1 Choose the correct option – one word or two separate words.

	a	b
1	a specialeffects	b special effects
2	a soundtrack	b sound track
3	a solarpower	b solar power
4	a bookcase	b book case
5	a sleepingbag	b sleeping bag
6	a housework	b house work

2 Write a compound word for the definitions.

1 A lane for bicycles to go in
cycle lane

2 A ring for keeping your keys on
____

3 Pads to protect your knees
____

4 Work from school to do at home
____

5 A dish for receiving satellite TV
____

6 Rings for your ears
____

➡ **Answers** page 116

8 ACTION!

VOCABULARY Film genres

1 Complete the film genres, and name one film in each genre.

Genre	Description	Examples
1 f antasy	Magic and the supernatural are important in these films.	*Pan's Labyrinth*
2 c ______	Charlie Chaplin was one of the first famous actors in this genre.	
3 th ______	These exciting films are often about spies or crime.	
4 r ______	The characters fall in love and there's usually a happy ending.	
5 d ______	These films show ordinary people and their lives.	*Mystic River*
6 w ______	The Navy, air force or army are shown in these films.	
7 m ______	They were popular in the 1950s and include singing and dancing.	
8 c ______	These films are about criminals and the justice system.	*American Gangster*

2 Write a description of these films genres.

1 Adventure films include a lot of action.

______

2 Animation films ______

______

3 Horror films ______

______

4 Science fiction films ______

______

3 Complete the sentences.

1 My favourite film genre is ______

because ______

2 I also like ______

because ______

3 I don't really like ______

because ______

4 I hardly ever watch ______

because ______

8

GRAMMAR Present and past passive: affirmative

1 Write sentences with the present passive. Can you put them in order?

6 steps to make a film

1 After that, the scenes / film
The scenes are filmed.

2 Finally the music / record
____

3 Then changes / make / during editing
____
____

4 First the script / write
____

5 Next the actors / contract
____

6 Then a producer / chose
____

The order *4*, _, _, _, _, _

2 Write the verbs in the past passive.

~~direct~~ give write play record win

1 The films *Gangs of New York* and *The Aviator* *were directed* by Martin Scorsese.
2 The role of Forrest Gump __________ by Tom Hanks.
3 David Beckham __________ a medal by the Queen of England in 2003.
4 The albums *Stripped* and *Back to Basics* __________ by Christina Aguilera.
5 The Oscar for best supporting actor __________ by Javier Bardem in 2008.
6 The Sherlock Holmes books __________ by Sir Arthur Conan Doyle

3 Complete the sentences in the past passive.

1 

2 

3 

4
$$\vec{F}_{12} = -G\frac{m_1 m_2}{|\vec{r}_1 - \vec{r}_2|^2}\hat{u}_{12}$$

1 *The Girl with the Pearl Earring* *was painted by Vermeer.* (paint / Vermeer)
2 *Ray of Light* and *American Life* __________ (sing / Madonna)
3 The telephone __________ (invent / Bell)
4 The Laws of Motion __________ (discover / Newton)

4 Write the verbs in the present or past passive.

The history of films

Moving pictures **(1)** __________ (present) to an audience for the first time by the Lumière Brothers in 1895. At first, films **(2)** __________ (show) at fairs or music halls and they didn't have sound. A film **(3)** __________ (accompany) by a lecture or music. The first film with sound was *The Jazz Singer* in 1927, and colour **(4)** __________ (add) to film in the 1930s.
Today, computer technology **(5)** __________ (use) in the production of a lot of films. And most films nowadays **(6)** __________ (see) on TV or computer screens and not at the cinema.

VOCABULARY – Behind the camera

1 Write the words. Then complete the famous film phrase.

1	D	[13] I	R	E	C	T	O	[9] R						
2						[14]								
3	[10]	[2]												
4		[16]			[17]		[11]							
5			[12]						[7]					
6		[8]				[4]								
7	[1]			[6]										
8		[5]								[15]	[3]			

[1] M [2] _ [3] _   [4] _ [5] _ [6] _   [7] _ [8] _ [9] _ [10] _ [11] _   B [12] _   W [13] _ [14] _ [15] _   [3] _ [16] _ [17] _

GRAMMAR – Present and past passive: negative

2 Write sentences with the present passive negative.

1 special effects – create by hand ✗ on a computer ✓

Special effects aren't created by hand; they're created on a computer.

2 a film review – write by a director ✗ by a journalist ✓

____

3 a video game – make after a film ✗ at the same time ✓

____

4 Oscars – give to sportspeople ✗ to actors ✓

____

3 Complete the sentences with the past passive negative. Each sentence eliminates one film. Which film are *all* the sentences about?

attack direct ~~film~~ make play set

1 The scenes *weren't filmed* on a ship.
2 The film ______________ in black and white.
3 It ______________ by George Lucas.
4 The characters ______________ by a monster.
5 It ______________ in Ancient Rome.
6 The main character ______________ by a Spanish actor.

Alien
The Legend of Zorro
Casablanca
Gladiator
Star Wars
The Matrix
~~*Titanic*~~

4 Write the verb in the present or past passive.

In a modern film, it's hard to know what's real and what isn't. Some dangerous scenes (**1**) *aren't filmed* (not film) on location – the location (**2**) ______________ (add) later using special effects. But, some dangerous action is real. In most cases, it (**3**) ______________ (not do) by an actor, but by a double called a *stuntman* or *woman*. But there are exceptions. Stuntmen (**4**) ______________ (not use) in Charlie Chaplin or Buster Keaton's films. And Tom Cruise (**5**) ______________ (not replace) by a stuntman in *Mission Impossible 3*. He did all the action scenes himself – but only after he (**6**) ______________ (give) permission by his wife.

Active v. passive

5 Circle the correct option.

1 The Sudoku puzzle *was invented* / *invented* by Howard Garns in 1979.
2 The German football team *didn't win* / *wasn't won* Euro 2008.
3 The sari *wears* / *is worn* by Indian women.
4 A Californian shop *built* / *was built* the first skateboard in 1958.
5 Independent films *don't produce* / *aren't produced* in Hollywood.

6 Write sentences in the active or passive.

1 Millions of people use Google every day.
Google *is used by millions of people every day.*
2 The Shrek films weren't produced by Disney.
Disney ______________
3 Bill Gates started Microsoft.
Microsoft ______________
4 Millions of objects are bought by eBay customers every year.
eBay customers ______________
5 China makes a lot of the world's clothes.
A lot of the world's clothes ______________

READING

1 Do the film quiz. Can you match the films with their titles?

Toy Story King Kong ~~Spider-Man 3~~ Alien Star Wars Tomb Raider

THE CONNECTIONS FILM QUIZ

This month's connection is video games! How many films can you name?

1 *Spider-Man 3*

Number three came out in 2003, and showed us the darker side of this friendly superhero. His fight against Sandman was also a popular video game.

2 ______

Today, many best-selling video games are based on films. This is an example of the opposite – a film based on a successful game, with Angelina Jolie in the leading role.

3 ______

Toys come to life in this 1995 classic. It was the first animation film produced entirely on a computer. The sequel opens with a scene from the Buzz Lightyear computer game.

4 ______

This legendary science fiction saga has six episodes. The fourth episode came out first, in 1977. Episodes one to three were released between 1999 and 2005.

5 ______

The original version came out in 1933, and the giant ape climbing the Empire State building is one of the greatest scenes in cinema history. A remake was made in 2005.

6 ______

This terrifying film about an alien on a spaceship was released in 1979. As the film's tag line says, 'In space no one can hear you scream.' A video game came out in 1982.

2 Match the sentences to the films.

1. It has more than four parts. *4*
2. It's a horror film set in space. _
3. It was made on computers. _
4. There's an old and a new version. _
5. We see a different aspect of the hero's personality. _
6. It came out after its video game. _

ENGLISH YOU NEED

1 Complete the dialogue with the words and phrases below.

don't recommend ~~really recommend~~
really must recommend should shouldn't

A It's John's party on Saturday. We should get him a present.

B Let's get a book. I (1) *really recommend* *Eragon* by Christopher Paolini.

A I've never heard of it.

B It's the best book I've ever read! You (2) ______________ read it! It's about a boy and his dragon.

A I don't think we (3) ______________ get him that. He doesn't like fiction. What about a biography?

B That's not a bad idea. But I (4) ______________ Andy Murray's biography. It's really disappointing.

A What do you (5) ______________?

B Maybe we (6) ______________ get a book. Maybe we should get a DVD instead.

A I know. Let's get him *Transformers*. It's a great film!

B OK. Let's get him that.

LISTENING

2 Tick (✓) if you agree.

1 If a film's based on a book, the book's always better than the film. _

2 A film's bad if its special effects are bad. _

3 Remakes are always better than the original film. _

3 15 Listen and answer the questions.

1 What film do John and Flo see?

____

2 Was it the original version or the remake?

____

4 15 Listen again and circle the correct options.

1 *Flo* / *John* loved the film.

2 *Flo* / *John* preferred the original version.

3 The original *was* / *wasn't* in colour.

4 The *original* / *remake* is three hours long.

5 Flo thinks the *acting* / *story* is better in the original version.

6 Flo *was* / *wasn't* happy to see the film.

DICTATION

5 16 Listen. Write six sentences about a film.

1 *It was* ______________

____

2 ______________

____

3 ______________

____

4 ______________

____

5 ______________

____

6 ______________

____

WRITING – A film review

1 Read the film review. Did the writer like the film? Why / Why not?

He ______________________________

____

Transformers

By K Evans

I wasn't sure about this film before I went to see it. It's based on a cartoon for kids, and it's also a video game. But my friends wanted to see it, so I went too. I loved it!

It's about a war between alien robots. The robots transform into ordinary machines on Earth. When Sam Witwicky buys his first car, he doesn't know it's really a robot.

Shia LaBeouf is excellent in the role of Sam and the plot is original as well. What's more, the special effects are the best I've ever seen. I definitely recommend it!

what's more, also, too, as well

2 Find these words in the review. Then circle the correct option.

1 I watch films at the cinema and on DVD *also* / *as well*.

2 I like musicals, animation and fantasy films *what's more* / *too*.

3 The costumes are amazing and the music's *also* / *too* great.

4 My favourite film's *Shrek*, but I like *Ratatouille* *as well* / *also*.

5 Johnny Depp's a great actor. *What's more* / *Too*, he can sing really well.

6 I liked Johnny Depp in the Pirates films and *also* / *too* in *Charlie and the Chocolate Factory*.

3 Write about a film you saw recently.

____

____

____

____

____

TRANSLATION

4 Translate the sentences.

1 My favourite film is *Notting Hill*.

____

2 The script was written by Richard Curtis.

____

3 It's set in London.

____

4 The songs were sung by famous singers.

____

5 I recommend this film because it's funny.

____

6 What's more, the plot's really good.

____

SELF CHECK 8

Film genres

1 Write the film genres. _ / 5

I love films about space travel, so my favourite film genre is (1) ____________. But I also like films with vampires and ghosts so my second favourite genre is (2) ____________ films. I'm a fan of Indiana Jones, and other (3) ____________ films. When I want to relax, I watch (4) ____________ films because I like humour. I don't like (5) ____________ films, because I don't like films with battles.

How things are done

2 Complete these sentences about making a music album. Use the present active or passive. _ / 5

1 First a band or singer ____________ (give) a contract by a recording company.

2 The band ____________ (not choose) the songs for the album, the producer does that.

3 Next the musicians ____________ (record) the album in a music studio.

4 At the same time, concert tours ____________ ____________ (plan).

5 The album ____________ (not release) until everything is ready to sell.

Who did it?

3 Write the verbs in the past active or passive. _ / 5

build   not paint   discover   not invent   write

1 The first electric light bulb ____________ ______ by Edison, but by Humphrey Davy.

2 The Ancient Egyptians ____________ their pyramids around 3000–2500 BC.

3 *The Da Vinci Code* and *Angels & Demons* ____________ by Dan Brown.

4 Some people think Goya ____________ the famous work *The Colossus*.

5 Penicillin ____________ by Alexander Fleming.

Make recommendations

4 Circle the correct option. _ / 5

A I'm going to buy Carla a CD for her birthday. What (1) *I should buy her / do you recommend*?

B Well, there's the Duffy CD. If you don´t know it, (2) *you must / I recommend* listen to it.

C I think you (3) *should / must* buy her a soundtrack. She loves the cinema.

B But she doesn't listen to soundtracks on CD. I (4) *shouldn't / don't think you should* buy her that.

A Maybe I should (5) *buy / to buy* her some earrings instead!

My favourite film

5 Choose the correct option. _ / 5

One of my favourite films is *Enchanted*. (1) ... cartoon characters in New York. The film starts as animation, but then in New York the characters (2) ... real people. But they dress like cartoon characters, and act like them (3) ... . (4) ... Amy Adams and Patrick Dempsey. I like it because the plot is original. (5) ..., it's really funny.

1	a It's about	b It treats
2	a play	b are played by
3	a as well	b also
4	a It's stars	b It stars
5	a Too	b What's more

➡ **Answers** page 118

9 Reference

COMMUNICATE

GRAMMAR

can, could, will be able to

can

Affirmative
I can
You can
He can
She can
It can
We can
You can
They can

Negative	
Full form	Contracted form
I cannot	I can't
You cannot	You can't
He cannot	He can't
She cannot	She can't
It cannot	It can't
We cannot	We can't
You cannot	You can't
They cannot	They can't

- *can* + infinitive is used to talk about ability in the present.
  She **can speak** several languages.
  He **can't cook** any meals.

could

Affirmative
I could
You could
He could
She could
It could
We could
You could
They could

Negative	
Full form	Contracted form
I could not	I couldn't
You could not	You couldn't
He could not	He couldn't
She could not	She couldn't
It could not	It couldn't
We could not	We couldn't
You could not	You couldn't
They could not	They couldn't

- *could* + infinitive is used to talk about ability in the past.
  Mr Jamieson **could sing** really beautifully when he was young.
  Rita **couldn't talk** until she was three.

will be able to

Affirmative	
Full form	Contracted form
I will be able to	I'll be able to
You will be able to	You'll be able to
He will be able to	He'll be able to
She will be able to	She'll be able to
It will be able to	It'll be able to
We will be able to	We'll be able to
You will be able to	You'll be able to
They will be able to	They'll be able to

Negative	
Full form	Contracted form
I will not be able to	I won't be able to
You will not be able to	You won't be able to
He will not be able to	He won't be able to
She will not be able to	She won't be able to
It will not be able to	It won't be able to
We will not be able to	We won't be able to
You will not be able to	You won't be able to
They will not be able to	They won't be able to

- *will be able to* + infinitive is used to talk about ability in the future.
  In a few years **we will be able to travel** to the Moon on holiday.
  We **won't be able to breathe** if pollution continues to increase.

1 Complete the sentences with *can/can't, could/couldn't* or *will/won't be able to.*

1. I can swim very well now but I couldn't swim when I was a child.
2. If you collect rainwater today, you ____________ use it to water plants tomorrow.
3. You ____________ watch TV now. You have to go to school.
4. My brother ____________ drive a car now because he's got a driving license.
5. The students ____________ use the computers next week because the computer room will be closed.
6. We ____________ play football because we found our ball.

➟ **Answers** page 116

Sense verbs

- To describe things we can see, feel, taste, hear and smell, we use the following structures:

  - *look, feel, taste, sound* and *smell* + adjective
  She **looks terrible**.
  That music **sounds** really **nice**.
  This chicken **doesn't smell** very good.

  - *look, feel, taste, sound* and *smell* + *like* + noun
  With her new haircut, Sarah **looks like a boy**.
  Try some – it **tastes like chicken**.
  What material is this? It **doesn't feel like silk**.

- *A* or *an* can only be used with countable nouns. We don't use them with uncountable nouns.
  Your cousin **looks like a film star**.
  This cake **tastes like coffee**.
  NOT … ~~tastes like a~~ coffee.

2 Add *like* if necessary.

1. Those flowers smell ________ wonderful.
2. Your cousin looks ________ beautiful.
3. That child's voice sounds ________ an angel.
4. What's this meat? It tastes ________ rabbit.
5. This material feels ________ cheap.
6. From a distance, it looks ________ a cheap vase.

➟ **Answers** page 116

9 Reference

VOCABULARY

Student's Multi-ROM Speaking dictionary

Communication

argue	/ˈɑːgjuː/	________
complain	/kəmˈpleɪn/	________
discuss	/dɪˈskʌs/	________
explain	/ɪkˈspleɪn/	________
gossip	/ˈgɒsɪp/	________
shout	/ʃaʊt/	________
tell	/tel/	________
whisper	/ˈwɪspə/	________

Sense verbs

feel excited	/fiːl ɪkˈsaɪtɪd/	________
look dangerous	/lʊk ˈdeɪndʒərəs/	________
look scared	/lʊk skeəd/	________
smell fresh	/smel freʃ/	________
sound terrible	/saʊnd ˈterəbl/	________
taste delicious	/teɪst dɪˈlɪʃəs/	________

English you need

- Offer help

Can I help you?

____

Thank you, but I can manage.

____

OK. That would be great.

____

Shall I clean the board for you?

____

That's very kind of you.

____

Would you like me to give out the homework?

____

It's all right, thanks.

____

Learning tip

- Puzzles are a good way to revise words.

1 Which word is different? Why?

					The others are …
1	earrings	necklace	(leggings)	ring	*jewellery*
2	canoeing	rafting	trekking	washing up	______
3	sculpture	architecture	cooking	painting	______
4	annoyed	frightened	excited	talk	______
5	waiter	charity	lawyer	vet	______
6	make-up	science fiction	fantasy	adventure	______

2 Make a puzzle. Include three related words and one different word.

1	*touristy*	*polluted*	crowded	*peaceful*
2	______	______	______	mop the floor
3	______	carefully	______	______
4	______	______	litter	______
5	bookcase	______	______	______
6	______	______	goggles	______

➡ **Answers** page 116

9 COMMUNICATE

VOCABULARY – Communication

1 Do the crossword.

(A)

(C)

(B)

(D)

Across

1 I think it's rude to *whisper* in someone's ear when you're with a group of friends. (7)

4 If I buy something and it doesn't work, I always go back to the shop to ______ (8)

6 Boys don't usually ______ about people and their personal lives. (6)

8 I ______ my best friend all my secrets. (4)

Down

2 My teacher can ______ grammar rules really well. (7)

3 My friends and I often ______ politics and other serious topics. (7)

5 I sometimes ______ with my parents about housework. (5)

7 It's really noisy in restaurants in my country because people don't talk, they ______ (5)

2 Describe the people in the pictures.

A *She's whispering in his ear.*

B ______

C ______

D ______

9

GRAMMAR – *can, could, will be able to*

1 Complete the sentences. Use *can, can't, could* and *couldn't* and the verbs.

play ride sing speak swim ~~talk~~

1 My parrot *can talk*. He says 'hello' and 'goodbye'.
2 When I was a child I had a bike, but I ______ it.
3 Jenny wants to be in the school musical, but ______ she ______ and dance?
4 My great-grandad loved travelling. He ______ French and Italian.
5 James isn't coming to the swimming pool. He ______
6 You play the piano really well. ______ you ______ well when you were a child?

2 Write sentences about the future with *will* and *won't be able to*.

1 we / choose / the colour of our baby's eyes
We'll be able to choose the colour of our baby's eyes.
2 scientists / not clone / human beings
______
3 doctors / not solve / all our health problems
______
4 they / find / a genetic solution for most of them
______
5 we / get / all our information from the Internet
______
6 we / not remember / much information
______

3 Read the article. Then complete the interview with Whitney's mum. Use *can, could* and *will be able to*.

There are many cases of animals helping children to overcome difficulties. Local girl Whitney is just one example.

Before Whitney met Magnolia, she needed a wheelchair to move about, and she didn't speak much. Horse-riding has given her another way to get around. Her muscles are getting stronger and her parents think she'll walk one day. Her speech has also improved.

A Before she met Magnolia, (1) *could Whitney speak*?
B Yes, but only a few words.
A (2) ______ without a wheelchair?
B No, she (3) ______
A (4) ______ alone, or is there an instructor with her?
B She rides alone, but she needs help to get on the horse.
A (5) ______ one day?
B Yes, she (6) ______. We're sure about that. Her muscles are getting stronger, and that's a very good sign.

VOCABULARY – Sense verbs

1 Complete the sense verbs.

1 'That l _ _ _ _ old-fashioned.'

2 'This t _ _ _ _ _ sour.'

3 'This f _ _ _ _ soft.'

4 'Your feet s _ _ _ _ terrible!'

5 'This talk s _ _ _ _ _ interesting.'

2 Find the adjectives from exercise 1, and 11 more.

A	Y	I	E	X	C	I	T	I	N	G	H	T
X	O	N	S	I	H	B	E	R	S	D	O	K
D	P	T	G	W	N	C	W	N	C	L	R	C
E	T	E	R	R	I	B	L	E	T	S	R	U
L	D	R	E	N	A	O	C	V	U	G	I	S
I	X	E	H	Y	B	N	M	O	A	E	B	C
C	O	S	W	E	E	T	R	F	O	Q	L	A
I	Q	T	S	K	M	E	F	L	R	L	E	R
O	P	I	H	O	G	R	L	Z	D	E	K	E
U	V	N	I	N	F	U	J	R	T	R	S	D
S	N	G	A	Z	D	T	A	B	U	F	J	H
O	L	D	F	A	S	H	I	O	N	E	D	E
F	Q	G	D	C	M	L	S	J	R	P	L	U

1 ____________ 7 ____________
2 ____________ 8 ____________
3 ____________ 9 ____________
4 ____________ 10 ____________
5 ____________ 11 ____________
6 ____________

GRAMMAR – Sense verbs

3 Complete the second part. Use a sense verb and an adjective.

dangerous delicious dull ~~horrible~~ nice scared

1 I hate my new haircut. It *looks horrible*!
2 Can I have another piece of your cake, please? It ______________________.
3 I don't listen to these Coldplay CDs anymore. I think they ______________________.
4 I like singing in public. I ______________________ before I start, but I love it.
5 I like perfumed candles. They make my room ______________________.
6 I never want to try rock-climbing. It ______________________.

4 Write sentences with a sense verb and *like*.

1 He looks like Brad Pitt.

3 My favourite perfume ______ roses.

2 The landscape ______ the surface of the moon

4 This jacket ______ real fur when you touch it.

5 Circle the correct option. Can you guess what it is?

1 It's a fruit. The skin (*feels*) / *feels like* hard.
2 I think it *looks* / *looks like* a head with hair on top.
3 It *smells* / *smells like* fresh when you cut it open.
4 Inside it *tastes* / *tastes like* sweet.
5 Part of the name *sounds* / *sounds like* another fruit.
6 But it doesn't *taste* / *taste like* that fruit.

a a melon **b** a banana **c** a pineapple

6 Complete the adverts with a sense verb and *like* if necessary.

Specs sunglasses

To protect your eyes and (**1**) look cool at the same time, wear the new Specs sunglasses. Specs are the latest fashion accessory in Hollywood, so if you want to (**2**) ______ a film star, wear Specs.

Exotic shower gel

Made with six citrus fruits, the Exotic shower gel (**3**) ______ lemons and oranges, and gives you a refreshing start to the day. Wash with Exotic, and your skin will (**4**) ______ soft and fresh all day.

Rosetti ice-cream

Yes, the name (**5**) ______ Italian, and the new Rosetti ice-creams (**6**) ______ home-made Italian ice-cream too. Try the chocolate fudge or the banana caramel. They're delicious!

7 Write your opinions of these things. Use sense verbs and adjectives.

Chinese food tattoos my shampoo theme park rides lettuce classical music

______

______

______

______

______

______

READING

1 What does the definition describe? Read the article and check your answer.

1 Braille **2** Sign language **3** Body language

> It's a way to communicate without sound.
>
> People make shapes, movements and gestures with their hands, face and body.
>
> It's mainly used by deaf people and other people with hearing difficulties.

2 Read again and complete the fact-file.

Name of language: **(1)** ____________________
Date of birth: **(2)** ____________________
Place of birth: **(3)** ____________________
Number of users: **(4)** ____________________

3 Answer the questions.

1 Why don't we know how and when most languages formed?
Because they're very old.

2 How many students attended the first programme for deaf children?
____

3 How did the students study Spanish?
____
____

4 Where did they create their language?
____

5 What did new students do to the language?
____
____

6 Why is this language special?
____
____

A new language is born!

Does this situation sound familiar? Somebody speaks to you in a foreign language. You don't understand. You start to use gestures. You do anything you can to communicate.

Languages are probably born this way. But because nearly all languages in the world are very old, nobody knows exactly how they formed. However, one language is less than 40 years old, and its users can tell us about its origins.

The story starts in 1977, when a school in the Managua region of Nicaragua opened a programme for fifty deaf children. By 1983 there were two schools, attended by 400 students. The schools tried to teach the children Spanish using lip reading and the alphabet. It didn't work, and there was little communication between teachers and students.

But something happened outside class. The children started to communicate. They used gestures and signs from home, and a simple new language started to form.

When new students arrived, they learned the language, and then improved it. It became more complex, and they could use it to express more ideas.

Today, it's officially called Nicaraguan Sign Language. There are around 3,000 signers and it's the world's youngest completely new language.

ENGLISH YOU NEED

1 Match the two parts of the offers.

1	Shall I	**a**	I help you?
2	I'll	**b**	to phone a doctor?
3	Can	**c**	find an assistant?
4	Would you like me	**d**	get you an aspirin.

2 Write the responses.

1 all right, / it's / thanks
It's all right, thanks.

2 would / great / that / be
____

3 but / I / manage / you, / thank / can
____

4 kind / of / very / you / that's
____

3 Complete with the offers and responses.

A (1) *Can I help you?*
B Thank you, but (2) ______________________________
____
A It's a very high shelf. (3) ______________________________
____
B Well, thank you. That (4) ______________________________
____

A I've got a terrible headache.
B (5) ______________________________
______________________________ doctor?
A It's (6) ______________________________. I'll be OK.
B (7) ______________________________
A That (8) ______________________________. Thanks.

LISTENING

4 17 Jackie's talking to a friend. Listen and answer the questions.

1 Who was she talking to before?
____

2 What did she say to him?
____

5 17 True or false? Correct the false sentences.

1 Jackie's brother is deaf.
False – her mother's deaf.

2 He can understand sign language.
____

3 Both of her parents are deaf.
____

4 Sign language is frustrating.
____

5 It was difficult to learn.
____

6 She sometimes feels frustrated when she communicates in sign language.
____

DICTATION

6 18 Listen. Write six sentences about Jackie's mother.

1 *My* ______________________________
____
2 ______________________________
____
3 ______________________________
4 ______________________________
____
5 ______________________________
6 ______________________________
____

WRITING – My plans

1 Match the words and phrases with a similar meaning.

1	talk	**a**	enormous
2	gigantic	**b**	fancy taking
3	very good	**c**	chat
4	relax	**d**	like
5	such as	**e**	chill out
6	want to take	**f**	great

2 Read the blog and write a word or phrase from a–f in exercise 1 in the spaces.

It's the end of term now. The last days at school are always more relaxed. On Friday, my friends and I bought an (1) enormous pizza and ate it in the park. It was (2) ________ because we could (3) ________ about our summer plans.

I can't wait for the holidays. I'll be able to get up late and (4) ________. Normally, I don't do anything but this year I (5) ________ a course in photography. They teach you things (6) ________ how to take portraits and develop photos.

Synonyms

3 Write a suitable synonym for the underlined words.

1 In August, we're going to stay in Wales.
In August, we're going to visit Wales.

2 I've heard that it's very nice.
____

3 I'll probably go to the beach and go hiking too.
____

4 I'm happy that we're not going abroad.
____

5 I'm not really into travelling now.
____

6 I hope everything's OK with you.
____

4 Write about now and your summer.

It's the end of term now.
____
____
____
____
____

CORRECTION

5 Correct the sentences.

1 My family and I discussed about summer plans. ✗
____
____

2 We're going to France. It sounds like great. ✗
____

3 I've told to my friends all about it. ✗
____

4 I'll can practise my French. ✗
____

5 Last year I couldn't to speak any French. ✗
____

6 Will I to send you a postcard? ✗
____

SELF CHECK

9

Communication

1 Complete the sentences with a communication verb. _ / 5

1 My sister and I are really good friends. We never ______________
2 Can you ______________ how to load a podcast onto my mp3 player?
3 My favourite classes are when we ______________ things in English.
4 If you don't want everyone to hear, ______________ in my ear.
5 You don't have to ______________! I'm not deaf.

Ability

2 Write the affirmative or negative of *can, could* or *will be able to*. _ / 5

Nowadays, most children (1) _________ use computers from an early age. But fifty years ago, computers were new inventions. Our grandparents (2) _________ look for information on the Internet. And computer technology is developing fast. Scientists believe that in the future, they (3) ______________________ upload the contents of our brains onto computers. At the moment, they (4) _________ do this, and they (5) ______________________ do it soon. But they believe that the technology will exist before the end of the century.

The senses

3 Complete the sentences with a sense verb and *like* if necessary. _ / 5

1 My dad loves singing but he's got a terrible voice. He ______________ a donkey.
2 I can't stand eating spinach. It _________ disgusting.
3 My family says that I ________________ my aunt. We've got the same eyes.
4 What are you cooking? It ________________ delicious!
5 It's really cold today. It's July but it ________________ winter.

Make offers

4 Complete the dialogue. _ / 5

A I have to finish this exercise. If I don't finish it, I won't be able to go out.
B (1) W _ _ _ _ y _ _ l _ _ _ m _ t _ help you?
A Yes, please. (2) T _ _ _ w _ _ _ _ b _ g _ _ _ _
B OK. What do you have to do?
A I have to find these capital cities.
B (3) S _ _ _ _ _ look for them on the Internet?
A Yes please. I'll switch the computer on.
B (4) I _' _ a _ _ _ _ _ _ _, t _ _ _ _ _
(5) I c _ _ m _ _ _ _ _

Summer plans

5 Circle the correct option. _ / 5

Thanks for your email, Tate. Your summer plans (1) *sound / sound like* great. Unfortunately, I (2) *couldn't / won't be able* to visit this year. My dad wants to take us to Ireland. It probably won't be exciting, but I mustn't (3) *gossip / complain*. I've heard that the scenery is really (4) *OK / beautiful*. (5) *Can I / I'll* get you a souvenir mug for your collection, if you like.
Love,
Mandy

➡ **Answers** page 118

Answers
Reference

Welcome

1
1 What club does he go to?
2 Correct
3 Which is your favourite film?
4 Correct
5 Correct
6 How often does your aunt visit?

2
1 don't like playing
2 doesn't like riding
3 like travelling
4 doesn't like going
5 likes riding
6 doesn't like playing

3
1 Where did you go on holiday?
2 I went to Disneyland.
3 Who was with you?
4 My parents were there.
5 What did they think of Disneyland?
6 They didn't like it.

Unit 1

1
1 loves following
2 can't stand following
3 doesn't mind creating
4 doesn't like creating
5 like wearing
6 hates shopping

2
1 is working
2 Do you go
3 I'm going
4 drives
5 doesn't like
6 I'm not watching

3
1 tall
2 later
3 the latest
4 hotter
5 the hungriest
6 more beautiful

4
1 What are those cakes like?
2 What's Paul like?
3 Correct
4 What's the weather like in Paris now?
5 Correct
6 What's the new baby like?

Learning tip
1
1 touristy
2 polluted
3 expensive
4 dangerous
5 authentic
6 peaceful

Sample answers: healthy, cheerful, long-sleeved, attractive, noisy, authentic, generous, messy, successful, crowded.

Unit 2

1
1 I don't have to go to bed early at the weekend.
2 My dad has to drive over 200 kilometres every day.
3 Students at my school have to learn German and French.
4 People don't have to wear a uniform in many jobs.
5 A film star doesn't have to wait at the bus stop.
6 Most people have to work hard all their lives.

2
1 b **2** e **3** a **4** f **5** d **6** c

3
1 can
2 don't have to
3 can't
4 don't have to
5 mustn't
6 don't have to

Learning tip
1
Students' own answers

2
Students' own answers

Unit 3

1
1 Did you go to the youth club last night?
2 No, I went to the cinema.
3 What did you see?
4 We saw the latest Harry Potter film.
5 What did you think of it?
6 I liked it a lot.

2
1 there were
2 There was
3 There wasn't
4 there was
5 there were
6 there weren't

3
1 fast
2 sadly
3 confidently
4 nervously
5 happily
6 slowly

4
1 was mopping
2 was talking
3 were studying
4 were watching
5 was chatting
6 wasn't raining

5
1 When I arrived home [S], my brother was listening to music and joking [S] with Tom.
2 They were telling jokes [S] while Georgia and I chatted [S] in the kitchen.
3 We were all talking very loudly [1] when there was a knock at the door [2].
4 When nobody answered the door, [1] the person knocked again [2].
5 We were all dancing [1] when the lights went out [2].
6 When a strange-looking man suddenly appeared at the back door [1] we got the shock of our lives [2].

Learning tip
1
1 cockroach
2 pavement
3 slowly
4 worried
5 landscape
6 self-portrait

2
Students' own answers

Unit 4

1
1 enough
2 too much
3 enough
4 too many
5 enough
6 too many

2
1 many
2 a lot of
3 some
4 a few
5 any
6 a little

Learning tip
1
1 a **2** b **3** b **4** b **5** a

2
Students' own answers

Unit 5

1
1 has been
2 hasn't been
3 haven't travelled
4 has travelled
5 have met
6 hasn't met

2
1 Has Jane ever cooked a meal for her family?
2 Have you been to the USA?
3 Where have Matt and Fiona moved to?
4 How often have you swum in the Mediterranean?
5 Have your parents bought a new car?
6 Have you ever seen a ghost?

3
1 Have they just arrived?
2 Peter's just left for school.
3 I've just seen Mary and Tony.
4 They've just been on holiday.
5 Has Alex just invited you to his party?
6 Have you just had a shower?

Learning tip
1
Students' own answers

2
Students' own answers

Unit 6

1
1 If you leave later, you'll miss the traffic.
2 If you eat something now, you won't be hungry later.
3 If you learn a foreign language, you'll get a better job.
4 If you give me your email address, we'll stay in contact.
5 If you don't go to bed too late, you won't be tired tomorrow.
6 If you don't listen, you won't understand the problem. / If you listen, you will understand the problem.

2
1 I'll call you when I get home.
2 Patricia will send me an email as soon as she arrives home.
3 I'll stay home until I finish my homework.
4 He'll put up the tent after we get to the campsite.
5 Dinner won't be ready before dad arrives.
6 She will wait until the film finishes.

3
1 'm going to
2 probably won't
3 might
4 will
5 will
6 probably won't

Learning tip
1
1 chairs: sofa, armchair
2 cards: library card, membership card
3 rubbish: litter, junk
4 tops: shirt, hoodie, sweatshirt

2
Students' own answers

Unit 7

1
1 has lived; for
2 have worked; since
3 hasn't seen; for
4 Have…talked; since
5 haven't had; since
6 have been; for

2
1 How long has Mark played football? ~ Since he was 7. (or For 25 years.)
2 How long has Mark liked art? ~ Since he was 13. (or For 19 years.)
3 How long has he known Cheryl? ~ Since he was 23. (or For 9 years.)
4 How long has he been a doctor? ~ Since he was 25. (or For 7 years.)
5 How long has he been married? ~ Since he was 26. (or For 6 years.)
6 How long has he had that watch? ~ Since he was 27. (or For 5 years.)

3
1 played
2 's played
3 didn't see
4 haven't seen
5 wore
6 've worn

Learning tip
1
1 knee pad
2 answer
3 write
4 island
5 honest
6 walked

2
1 climb
2 listen
3 ironing
4 knock
5 building
6 vegetable

Unit 8

1
1 The play is based on a famous novel.
2 Correct
3 This watch was repaired last Christmas.
4 Correct
5 The sandwich was eaten by Pam.
6 This car was built by robots.

2
1 The play isn't based on a famous novel.
2 The man wasn't seen in various parts of town.
3 This watch wasn't repaired last Christmas.
4 Some actors aren't only chosen for their good looks.
5 The sandwich wasn't eaten by Pam.
6 This car wasn't built by robots.

3
1 Many Egyptian artefacts were stolen.
2 Several awards were won by this actor last year.
3 The truth wasn't told by William.
4 Many royal portraits were painted by Holbein.
5 The watch was bought by a foreign collector.
6 Tarmac was invented by John McAdam.

Learning tip
1
1 b 2 a 3 b 4 a 5 b 6 a

2
1 cycle lane
2 key ring
3 knee pads
4 homework
5 satellite dish
6 earrings

Unit 9

1
1 couldn't
2 will be able to
3 can't
4 can
5 won't be able to
6 could

2
1 –
2 –
3 like
4 like
5 –
6 like

Learning tip
1
1 leggings – jewellery
2 washing up – adventure sports
3 cooking – types of art
4 talk – adjectives for emotions
5 charity – jobs
6 make-up – film genres

2
Students' own answers

Answers
Self Check

Unit 1

1
1 trousers
2 long-sleeved
3 earrings
4 belt
5 sweatshirts

2
1 'm studying
2 gives
3 don't have
4 play
5 are coming

3
1 wettest
2 more peaceful
3 cleaner
4 more cosmopolitan
5 liveliest

4
1 of
2 's
3 Do
4 Do
5 are

5
1 follow
2 mind
3 wearing
4 shopping
5 stand

Unit 2

1
1 does
2 mops
3 take out
4 lays
5 make

2
1 have to
2 don't have to
3 do … have to
4 has to
5 don't have to

3
1 can't/mustn't ride
2 don't have to use
3 don't have to buy
4 mustn't make
5 can learn

4
1 How's it going?
2 What are you up to?
3 Loads
4 Do you fancy
5 Hang on

5
1 parents
2 don't
3 sister's
4 parents'
5 its

Unit 3

1
1 loudly
2 well
3 angrily
4 carefully
5 patiently

2
1 There was
2 there weren't
3 Were there
4 there were
5 there wasn't

3
1 painted
2 was living
3 was renting
4 were using
5 wanted

4
1 shall we
2 Why don't we
3 That's a terrible idea.
4 How about
5 That sounds great.

5
1 when
2 At first
3 later
4 were making
5 eventually

Unit 4

1
1 traffic
2 pollution
3 cycle lanes
4 recycling bins
5 solar panels

2
1 've got too much
2 are too many
3 haven't got enough
4 aren't enough
5 make too much

3
1 much
2 a little
3 many
4 a few
5 any

4
1 an amazing
2 terrifying
3 good
4 disgusting
5 delicious

5
1 exciting
2 them
3 interested
4 it
5 boring

Unit 5

1
1 vet
2 engineer
3 social worker
4 architect
5 journalist

2
1 's made
2 've forgotten
3 haven't heard
4 's sold
5 Have … seen

3
1 been
2 just
3 ever
4 never
5 gone

4
1 membership
2 entry
3 do you have
4 to
5 does it cost

5
1 chef
2 had
3 his sense of humour
4 I've never
5 because

Unit 6

1
1 chest of drawers
2 bedside table
3 armchair
4 chair
5 blind

2
1 'll see; clean
2 won't sleep; 's got
3 are; 'll feel
4 don't open; won't come
5 've got; 'll disturb

3

1 'm going to
2 will
3 will probably
4 might
5 probably won't

4

1 along
2 turning
3 keep
4 turn
5 on

5

1 However
2 On the one hand
3 might
4 On the other hand
5 In conclusion

Unit 7

1

1 stick
2 helmet
3 pads
4 gloves
5 skates

2

1 haven't changed
2 since
3 has become
4 about a hundred years
5 since

3

1 How long have you known
2 met
3 How long has she been
4 hasn't lived
5 came

4

1 to change
2 wrong
3 work
4 about
5 receipt

5

1 like
2 such as
3 for example
4 autograph book
5 scarf

Unit 8

1

1 science fiction
2 horror
3 adventure
4 comedy
5 war

2

1 is given
2 don't choose
3 record
4 are planned
5 isn't released

3

1 wasn't invented
2 built
3 were written
4 didn't paint
5 was discovered

4

1 do you recommend
2 you must
3 should
4 don't think you should
5 buy

5

1 It's about
2 are played by
3 as well
4 It stars
5 What's more

Unit 9

1

1 argue
2 explain
3 discuss
4 whisper
5 shout

2

1 can
2 couldn't
3 will be able to
4 can't
5 will be able to

3

1 sounds like
2 tastes
3 look like
4 smells
5 feels like

4

1 Would you like me to
2 That would be great.
3 Shall I
4 It's all right, thanks.
5 I can manage.

5

1 sound
2 won't be able to
3 complain
4 beautiful
5 I'll

Irregular verbs

Infinitive	Past simple	Past participle
be	was/were	been
beat	beat	beaten
become	became	become
begin	began	begun
bite	bit	bitten
break	broke	broken
bring	brought	brought
build	built	built
buy	bought	bought
catch	caught	caught
choose	chose	chosen
come	came	come
cost	cost	cost
cut	cut	cut
do	did	done
draw	drew	drawn
dream	dreamt/dreamed	dreamt/dreamed
drink	drank	drunk
drive	drove	driven
eat	ate	eaten
fall	fell	fallen
feed	fed	fed
feel	felt	felt
fight	fought	fought
find	found	found
fly	flew	flown
forget	forgot	forgotten
freeze	froze	frozen
get	got	got
give	gave	given
go	went	gone
grow	grew	grown
have	had	had
hear	heard	heard
hide	hid	hidden
hit	hit	hit
hold	held	held
keep	kept	kept
know	knew	known

Infinitive	Past simple	Past participle
lay	laid	laid
learn	learnt/learned	learnt/learned
leave	left	left
let	let	let
lose	lost	lost
make	made	made
mean	meant	meant
meet	met	met
pay	paid	paid
put	put	put
read	read	read
ride	rode	ridden
ring	rang	rung
run	ran	run
say	said	said
see	saw	seen
sell	sold	sold
send	sent	sent
shoot	shot	shot
show	showed	shown
shut	shut	shut
sing	sang	sung
sink	sank	sunk
sit	sat	sat
sleep	slept	slept
smell	smelt/smelled	smelt/smelled
speak	spoke	spoken
spend	spent	spent
stand	stood	stood
steal	stole	stolen
swim	swam	swum
take	took	taken
teach	taught	taught
tell	told	told
think	thought	thought
understand	understood	understood
wear	wore	worn
win	won	won
write	wrote	written